Cyril Ray's Book of Wine

William Morrow and Company, Inc.
New York

Cyril Ray's Book of Wine

ABOVE *Wine tasting in Valdepeñas, Spain.*

Originally published as *The Guide to Wine* by Artus Publishing Company Limited, 11 St John's Hill, London SW11, England

Library of Congress Catalog Card Number 78-53517   ISBN 0-688-03333-4

Designed by Graham Dudley
Printed in Great Britain by Jarrold and Sons Ltd, Norwich
Colour separations by Radstock Reproductions
Maps by D.P. Press Ltd

Contents

What Wine is and What it's For

From vine to glass — the technique of wine-making has changed little throughout its history.

A Word About Wine

OPPOSITE *These vines at Romanée will produce one of the greatest red Burgundies, from the classic Pinot Noir grape.*

THERE IS NO MYSTERY ABOUT WINE. IT IS ONE OF THE MOST NATURAL beverages in the world, one of the oldest and one of the most wholesome, just as cheese is one of the oldest and most natural and most wholesome foods.

There are many official definitions but that laid down by the Wine and Spirit Association of Great Britain is used here because it is more precise:

Wine is the alcoholic beverage obtained from the juice of freshly gathered grapes, the fermentation of which has been carried through in the district of its origin, and according to local tradition and practice.

So home-made derivatives of other fruits, or vegetables or flowers, may be delicious (I have tasted a very agreeable drink made from elder-flowers) but are not wine, nor is any beverage that began as wine but has been de-alcoholised – there are German products of the sort that are useful at breaks in long motor-car drives, but they do not keep, and they are not wine. Neither is British 'wine' made from raisins or from imported concentrates, though the wine made in English vineyards from the grapes they grow is as genuine as the noblest claret, or as wine made in California from French varieties of grape grown in California.

BELOW *Two red and one white Burgundy (the great Montrachet) from the slopes of the Côte de Beaune.*

Just as there is no mystery about wine, so there should be no mystique. It is not meant to be a status symbol, or a means by which snobs can show off their superior knowledge. It is meant to be enjoyed, and anyone can enjoy it who is able to distinguish the smell of lavender, say, from that of a lemon, who can match a cushion with the curtains, and has enough sense of taste to know whether he or she is eating a sardine or a sole, a strawberry or a raspberry.

A sense of smell, a sense of taste, an eye for colour – all else is experience and personal preference. Just as we learn the differences between apples and pears, beef and mutton, trout and turbot, by eating them, so we learn to know the differences between claret and Chianti, port and sherry, by drinking them. From the moment one becomes interested in wine, one never stops learning, and it is when one has learned a few basic differences between types of wine – this one is red, that one is white; this is still, that one sparkles; some are dry, some are sweet, some not quite either – that one can begin to indulge one's own tastes, and partner this dish with that bottle.

There are no rules to be learned before making such choices. The only rule about wine-drinking is to drink what you like. Obviously, though, the more wines you taste, the more choices you can make, and the more interesting your choices will become.

You can add to your own experience that of your forefathers. For, although there are no laws about wine-drinking, there is a great deal of accumulated experience, and when you read in books, or hear from the experts, maxims such as 'white wine cool and with fish', 'red wine at room temperature and with red meat', do not dismiss it out of hand as wine-snobbery. These are not tablets of the law brought down by some

gastronomic Moses, but the collective wisdom of the ages telling us – just as it tells us that mustard goes better than marmalade with beef – that for most people, at any rate, there is some sort of chemical reaction between red wine and fish that leaves a metallic taste in the mouth; that white wine is more refreshing if served cellar-cool, but flabby at room temperature; whereas that is the temperature at which red wine shows off its fragrance and fruitiness.

But there is no reason why we should not try for ourselves and, if we disagree with our grandfathers, drink our champagne warmed up a bit, our burgundy on the rocks, and wash down kippers or clams with vintage port.

All that this book aims to do is to pass on some of the age-old wisdom about wine, not as gospel but as a guide, and to sketch in some of the history of the beverage in the bottle, and something about the places it may have come from, chiefly to dispel the air of mystery that sometimes seems to surround what ought to be, in Shakespeare's words, 'a good familiar creature'.

The Vine has Deep Roots

THE BOOK OF GENESIS SAYS OF NOAH THAT HE 'BEGAN TO BE AN husbandman, and he planted a vineyard.' The Bible may not be the most authoritative source of historical fact, but it does suggest that to the ancient Hebrews of years ago, which is when Genesis is supposed to have been written, the origins of wine-growing were already lost in the mists of time. Well they might have been.

Long before Genesis was written, wine was being made in Babylon and, long before Christ, the Egyptians made Osiris their god of wine (Dionysus was his Greek, and Bacchus his Roman counterpart); and that mysterious people, the Etruscans, who were making wine in what is now Chianti country before the Romans came to Rome, had a god of vineyard and vat called Fufluns. The Greeks took the vine, and the craft of wine-making, to the south of France; in southern Italy they found the vine already established, but made better wine than the local people had known how to.

But the history of wine as we know it today begins with the Romans. In Rome's golden age – from a couple of hundred years before Christ to a couple of hundred years after – the Romans imported fine wines from the Greek islands and from Spain, as well as growing red wines and white, sweet wines and dry, in vineyards of their own. They knew about the scientific training and pruning of vines, and they knew about ageing the finest of their products, probably in earthenware jars, sealed with plaster, and marked with the year of the vintage.

Early viticulture: Noah digging in his vineyard. A fifteenth-century stained-glass window in Great Malvern Priory.

The poet Martial, who lived in Nero's time, one thousand nine hundred years ago, wanted to kiss 'lips moist with old Falernian' (the most celebrated wine of Ancient Rome) and, in the same period, when the *nouveau riche* Trimalchio and his wife, Fortunata, wanted to impress their guests it was a hundred-year-old Falernian that Trimalchio clapped his hands over, crying 'Alas, that wine lives longer than man! Let's wet our whistles – wine is life!'

Wherever the Roman legions trod, there grew, and there still grows, the grape. After a lapse of many centuries, it grows again in Britain, in Hampshire and the Isle of Wight, Lincolnshire, Kent and Suffolk. This is as far north as drinkable wine can be grown, as the vine grows only in a temperate climate. In the northern hemisphere it is grown as far south as Africa, but only those areas north of the Sahara. In the similarly temperate zone of the southern hemisphere, wine is grown in South Africa, South America, Australia and New Zealand.

But ever since Roman times, Western Europe has been the homeland of wine. It may not be so for ever: the Soviet Union, the United States, Canada, Australia and Argentina are all expanding their wine-growing areas, and establishing experimental vineyards and modern wineries. But Italy, France, Spain, Portugal and Germany produce between them more than half the world's wine, and set the standards by which the rest of the world's table wines, fortified wines and sparkling wines are judged. It is not only that they have the soil, the vines and the climates that combine to make good wine – they also have centuries of experience and of inherited skills.

Trade follows the flag. As the Roman soldiers and then the Italian traders pushed north and west along the French and German river valleys they found that these northerly latitudes produced more delicate wines than most

The grape harvest, fourth century AD. Note the treading of grapes, a technique that goes back to pre-biblical Egypt, and survived until our own time. This vault mosaic is in Santa Constanza, in Rome.

ABOVE *The ancient Romans stored their wine in earthenware amphorae, like these in the Carthaginian port of Salammbo.*

RIGHT *This detail from a sixteenth-century French tapestry shows the vintage in the Loire – some grapes being pressed, some trodden.*

of those of the Mediterranean. Strains of vine were developed that suited the climate and the soil of each region, and, as one of the great rivers had at its mouth a Mediterranean port, Marseilles, and the other an Atlantic port, Bordeaux, the wines could be exported north and south to where Roman soldiers and civil servants were demanding them – and teaching their new neighbours to do so too.

With the spread of Christianity, monastery vineyards produced wine for sacramental purposes. Throughout the Dark Ages the Church, and laymen too, preserved the skills of wine-making, and it was pagan barbarians from the east who cleared the forests of Burgundy, the country named after them, to create vineyards. Clearing forests for vineyards also made timber available for cask-making, and wooden casks are better for shipping wine than the earthenware jars of the ancient Romans.

When Henry II came to the English throne in 1154 he was already married to Eleanor of Aquitaine, who brought with the marriage the greatest wine-growing region of France, the south-west, with La Rochelle and Bordeaux as its ports. For three hundred years, until Joan of Arc inspired her countrymen to drive out the English, the wines of the region reached English ports easily and, through them, Scandinavian and Baltic and Hanseatic merchants. This established for French wines a world-wide prestige that they have never lost. English wines went out of production because it was easier and cheaper to import from France. Back from the Baltic and the Hanseatic ports came the wines from the Rhine, so that 'Rhenish', the wine of that region, was known to Shakespeare and drunk both by Cromwell and by Charles II.

These were all table wines, but by this time, as will be seen in later chapters, the Spaniards had fortified the dry white wines of their deep south into sherry, and the Portuguese enriched the fuller reds of their north country into 'the Englishman's wine' – port.

Spaniards took the vines of Europe to California and to Chile; Huguenots took them to the Cape; and, almost two hundred years ago, an English sea-captain and an Anglican missionary took them to the Antipodes. Eventually, the New World was to repay the debt. In the 1860s, the phylloxera, the vine-louse, began its deadly work in the south of France, and by the end of the century had swept Europe. Europe's vines were saved by grafting them on to native American vine-roots, resistant to the parasite, and now virtually all the best wines in the world, from the Crimea to California, are made from the classic French and German varieties of vine grafted on to American roots.

How Wine is Made

THE JUICE IN THE GRAPE IN THE VINEYARD BECOMES THE WINE IN THE bottle on the table by a perfectly natural process, but one that is *controlled* by man. Man does away with pests and diseases in the vineyard; he decides what varieties of grape suit what sort of soil and what climate; and in some countries (though the wine laws forbid it in others) he exercises some sort of control even over the climate by irrigation and, in California, by installing

overhead sprinklers – rainfall on demand.

Man determines by temperature control whether to let the juice ferment quickly or slowly; whether to check it before it is complete and thus leave some natural sweetness in the finished wine, or to let the grape-sugar all ferment into alcohol; he can take the juice of black grapes away from the skins at once, and make white wine; fairly quickly and make rosé; or not until the pigmentation in the skins has made it a deep, rich red. He can pasteurise, and he can filter or get rid of impurities by 'fining' – by, that is, allowing a film of isinglass or egg-white to sink through the fermented juice, carrying unwanted solids to the bottom.

Despite the fact that man *controls* the transformation of a fruit-juice into an alcoholic beverage, he does not alter or adulterate. He does not colour the wine – the pigment in the skins does that – and he does not flavour (except for vermouths). And in all the major wine-growing countries the law of the land rigidly regulates what grape may be used for which wine, how the vine

Selecting grapes for picking at vintage-time in the Loire valley.

Stages in the production of wine:
ABOVE Grapes being taken to the press at the champagne cellar, Epernay. Generally grapes are fed into a crusher-stemmer (or égrappoir) which tears off the stalks and pumps the broken grapes into a press.

RIGHT Grapes are in the press, and wine is on its way.

OPPOSITE ABOVE The next stage: the must (or fresh juice) of black grapes fermenting in Valdepeñas, Spain – which means that it will soon be wine.

OPPOSITE BELOW To make red wine the skins of the grapes are left in for a while to give colour. Here the skins are being separated from the wine.

20

shall be pruned and trained, what fertilisers and insecticides may be used, and how much wine it may produce; whether and when sugar may be added before fermentation, not to sweeten, but to increase alcoholic strength and, thus, staying power; what minimum strength must be attained; and even the date of the vintage.

It is the wild yeasts present in the 'bloom' on the grape that cause fermentation, and this tumultuous bubbling of the juice lasts anything from three or four days to three or four weeks, depending on the surrounding temperature. Sometimes, in cool or coldish climates, fermentation is not complete when winter checks it, and there will be a tendency for it to begin again in the spring. As will be seen in the chapter on champagne, this tendency can be encouraged, to produce a sparkling wine.

(There are other methods of producing sparkling wine. The cheapest is to pump gas into white wine to make it fizz like ginger-beer or tonic-water. A more respectable method is to induce in big tanks the secondary fermentation that in the classic champagne method takes place in the bottle, and then bottle under pressure. This latter method can produce sound, refreshing sparklers, but they are not champagne, and may not be so described.)

For most still table wines – the usual red or white or rosé we drink with meals – fermentation is allowed to run its full course, so that all natural grape-sugar is converted into alcohol, and the finished wine will be dry.

Fermentation can be arrested by the addition of spirit such as brandy, and this is how port is made – a rich wine retaining much of the natural sweetness of the fruit.

The other well-known fortified wine is sherry. Here, though, the brandy is added after fermentation, to strengthen and preserve. Sherry is dry by nature: sweet, dessert sherries are made by blending in the juice of grapes that have been dried virtually into raisins.

Unfortified sweet dessert wines, such as Sauternes, are made by picking grapes so very ripe, even overripe, that there is more sugar in the juice than the yeasts can cope with: fermentation finishes of its own accord without having to be arrested, and the wine remains naturally sweet.

A few wines are made to be drunk very young indeed – Beaujolais nouveau is the classic example – but most have at least a few months in maturing casks or vats, and then more time in the bottle. The very finest vintage ports and clarets need ten years or so of bottle-age, and grower, shipper and merchant alike all prefer the consumer to stand the capital costs of putting them away. These are the wines listed by wine-merchants as 'for laying down'. Generally speaking it can be assumed that a wine on sale is ready for drinking, though all wines will keep; cheap red wines always repay a few months more bottle-age after purchase, and fortified wines, unopened, keep pretty well indefinitely.

Finally, a word about vermouth, the exception I mentioned in my statement earlier that we do not flavour wines: it is a red or a white wine flavoured with herbs and/or spices, fortified with spirit, sweetened or kept dry. We shall meet it again in my next chapter.

Wine With and Without Food

Château Haut-Brion comes from the Graves area, known chiefly for its white wines, but this red wine has the rare distinction of being classed as a 'first growth', the only red Bordeaux wine to achieve this outside the Haut-Médoc.

Before and Between Meals

ABOVE *The tulip-shaped glass, considered to be the best for preserving the bouquet of the wine, shows off the limpidity and sparkle of champagne.*

THERE ARE THOSE (AND I MUST CONFESS TO BEING ONE OF THEM) WHO like a glass of something cold and bubbly, not necessarily the most expensive champagne, to freshen the palate and sharpen the appetite before a meal, or to break the monotony of a Sunday morning. Some need the buck-you-up effect, after a hard day at the office or the launderette, of a mixed drink based on gin or vodka, or a stiff whisky-and-soda. But 'fizz' is not always feasible, and this book is about wine, not about the hard stuff, which is not to say that I have not known occasions when a five-to-one dry Martini has justified God's ways to man. In any case, too much spirits or over-strong mixtures deaden the palate for the food that follows and, especially, for the wine that goes with it. To the true wine-lover the best aperitif – which is simply a fancy name for an appetiser – is sherry, vermouth, or a glass of cool white wine.

What sort of sherry to choose is partly a matter of circumstances – even of climate, but chiefly, and as always with wine, a matter of taste. The driest kind of sherry is the fino, sometimes simply referred to as a 'pale' or as a 'dry' sherry. Manzanilla is a sort of local variant. Amontillado is fuller in colour and in flavour, and is almost certainly what you will get if you ask for a 'medium' sherry.

I would serve a fino, a pale sherry (or a Manzanilla) before a meal, but an amontillado, or medium, at a Sunday morning sherry party at which snacks are served. Both should be served cool but, if we are going to be pernickety about it, the fino perhaps the cooler. And on very cold days a medium sherry is more comforting than a fino. ('Cream' or 'golden' or 'old brown' or oloroso sherries are rich and sweet, and made to be served like port, as dessert wines: we shall discuss them in a later chapter.)

Spain is the only country entitled to the name 'sherry' in its own right. After all, it is named after the southern-Spanish town of Jerez, pronounced 'Herreth'. There is a word or so about how it is made in the later chapter on Spain. Other countries, though, produce wines of the same sort that may legally be named 'sherry' so long as the name of the country of origin is displayed with equal prominence. Cyprus, in particular, produces some admirable sherries, cheaper than those of Spain, but their driest examples are not so easy to find as the sweetest.

Sherry is a fortified wine, which is to say that brandy has been added in the course of its production, and makes it about half as strong again to twice as strong, in terms of alcohol, as ordinary red or white table wines. This is why it is served in smaller glasses, and why it will keep in good heart after the bottle has been opened. It will last days and even weeks (the more delicate finos, though, not so long as the fuller-bodied amontillados) especially if the bottle is kept in the fridge or a cold cellar tightly corked or, better still, if the sherry is poured into a smaller bottle so that as little air-space as possible is left between wine and cork. The fuller sherries, unopened, keep for many months – even years – in the cellar, and the delicate finos and such for at any rate a few months: in these days of rising prices it is worth keeping a modest reserve.

All of which is just as true of vermouth – it is fortified; it is stronger than

OPPOSITE *Sherry casks at Jerez de la Frontera, under the sub-tropical palm trees in southern Spain. On the main road from Seville to Cadiz, this area produces the only wine entitled to be called 'sherry'.*

A glass of 'French' vermouth, served cool and with a slice of lemon, is a welcome appetizer on a summer day, or mixes well with gin or vodka.

table wine; it should be served cool; and it will keep. Vermouth is basically a white wine, strengthened with spirit and made aromatic with herbs. Traditionally, the two main types are 'French' (dry white) and 'Italian' (sweet red) but both types are now made in each country and, to make confusion worse confounded, there is a sweet as well as a dry white.

Although best known in Britain and the United States as a mixer, with gin or with vodka, vermouth was meant to be taken, and is drunk by the French and Italians who make it, neat, perhaps with a twist of lemon peel in it. Ideally it should be served ice-cold, preferably by keeping the bottle in the fridge rather than gradually diluting the flavour and diminishing the effect by putting a piece of ice in the glass.

Cheaper than either sherry or vermouth is a glass of cool white wine, which makes a splendid palate-cleanser before a meal – dry (such as an Alsace or a white burgundy); similarly dry but fuller (such as a Graves); not quite so dry (a German, Hungarian or Yugoslav riesling) but not sweet (such as a Sauternes) which is better with fruit *after* the meal. With about half or a quarter as much soda splashed into it, it is especially crisp and refreshing on a hot day, and not all that far removed from the hock-and-seltzer with which the men-about-town of Oscar Wilde's time whetted their jaded appetites.

With a spoonful or so to taste of blackcurrant cordial it approximates to the *vin blanc cassis* (you can make a *vermouth-cassis* the same way, using a dry white vermouth) which the people of Burgundy, using the richly sweet, fortified *crème de cassis* of the region, call 'un Kir', after a much-loved Canon Kir who was the sturdily left-wing, patriotic mayor of Lyons during the German occupation. What better memorial can a man have than a drink named after him?

White Wines with Meals

ONE ADVANTAGE OF SIMPLY SERVING COOL WHITE WINE AS A BEFORE-dinner appetiser is that you can go on serving the same wine with the first course. 'Bring your glasses with you', says host or hostess as the guests are called to the table, and whatever cool white wine they are already drinking – dry or not quite so dry, so long as it is not fully sweet – will go well with avocado or pâté, potted shrimps or smoked salmon, at the beginning of a meal. (Not with soup, though. There are those who advise a dry sherry or a dry madeira with soup, but most people these days, I think, agree with me that liquid does not need a liquid accompaniment – though a glass of madeira poured *into* turtle soup is hallowed by tradition. Neither the one nor the other is all that frequent these days, except at City banquets.)

But if the main, or the only, course is a full-flavoured fish dish, perhaps with a rich sauce, then many people would like a rather fuller-flavoured wine than the one drunk before the meal. A sound, dry white wine will go with anything, with meat as well as with fish, but may well seem insipid if the food is rich. For instance, there would seem little taste in most dry white burgundies if partnered with jugged hare, or braised oxtail, or roast beef with all the trimmings. Or, for that matter, with salmon and mayonnaise, which seems to call for a fuller wine.

Whatever one's own tastes, and I have already proclaimed that one should drink what one likes and how one likes it, one must assume that guests' tastes will be conventional, and serve wines accordingly – white with fish, red with meat. With this in mind, remember that when choosing wine, chicken counts as fish, and so does rabbit, but hare is meat, and so are game-birds. Turkey is either, according to how richly it is served. This is not so madly arbitrary as the statement of the railway porter in the old *Punch* joke explaining to the bewildered passenger what animal he had to buy a ticket for and what not: 'Cats is dogs, and rabbits is dogs, and so's Parrats, but this 'ere Tortis is a insect, and there ain't no charge for it. . . .'

It is really a matter of the colour of the bird or beast concerned and, when in doubt, the richness of the sauce or the accompaniments. Thus, as to that debatable bird, the turkey, I should be inclined to serve a red wine with roast turkey accompanied with a savoury stuffing, forcemeat or sausages, roast potatoes and whatever, but a white wine with turkey done according to a Victorian recipe I came across the other day – boiled, with celery sauce – or

Full, fruity and fragrant, Johannisberger, from one of the sunniest stretches of the Rhine, is a wine to linger over on a summer's evening.

27

with slices of cold turkey breast on Boxing Day.

On the whole, the drier, crisper white wines go best with fish. Wines from the Loire, such as Muscadet and Sancerre, go especially well with shellfish, as does Chablis. Soave, from near Verona, and Verdicchio, from the Adriatic coast, are Italian whites that are usually served with the fish-fries of Venice, and very enjoyable, too. There are some who say that red wine goes with red fish, such as salmon, or red mullet, but my own choice would be a rather fuller white, such as one of the more expensive, 'bigger', white burgundies, or a German wine – remembering of the latter that hock (Rhine) in its brown bottle, is rather fuller and slightly less dry than the more delicate Moselle, in its green bottle.

All white wines show themselves at their best if served cellar-cool, or after an hour or so in the fridge. If anything, although one can be too fussy in these matters, the sweeter the wine, the colder.

Sweet white wines come into their own with the pudding course, or with fruit. Never, though, allow them to become quite so cold as to freeze out the flavour completely, or to numb the palate so that it cannot taste at all, which I suppose amounts to the same thing. The classics are Sauternes and Barsacs from France, and those very rich hocks, from Germany, that are made from late-gathered grapes. There used at one time to be a silly, snobbish prejudice against sweet wines, but the people who grow and make them know better, and any Frenchman will tell you how delicious a glass of Sauternes is with a ripe peach after dinner. And, when raspberries are in season, raspberries and cream served with a glass of Barsac (the near neighbour of Sauternes, in the Bordeaux area) is a delightful combination.

The great thing about these lusciously sweet white wines is (I stress once more) to serve them very cold, and in smallish amounts. Use the same sort of glass in which you serve dry white wines with fish or with chicken, but only half full, instead of about two-thirds, so that there is room in which to capture the very appealing fragrance of a sweet wine, and to dip one's nose into it, but not so much rich, golden liquid as to cloy.

Red Wines with Meals

THE WORLD'S TWO BEST-KNOWN AND MOST WRITTEN-ABOUT RED WINES are both French – claret, which is the red wine of the Bordeaux region, and burgundy. They are the wines by which other red wines are judged, and in terms of which they are described, so that in the old days, before the names were legally protected, labels and advertisements might proclaim 'Australian burgundies' and 'Chilean clarets', and one described this or that red wine by saying it was more like claret, or was of a burgundy type.

The reason, though, for their always being compared and contrasted is that there is not really all that much difference or, to put it another way, that the difference is so narrow that one has to go into a great deal of detail to define it. It is much less marked than that, say, between beef and mutton. It can be said, and every writer about wine has to say it some time, that at their most typical claret is the lighter and more delicate of the two, burgundy

OPPOSITE *'White wine with fish . . .' Not an old wives' tale: many people find that red wine with fish seems to produce a metallic taste in the mouth. An Italian fish looks reproachfully at the white Frascati, from near Rome, that will wash him down.*

29

OPPOSITE *Côtes du Rhône has the right sort of richness to go with a savoury casserole of lamb. The appellation Côtes du Rhône is a general one for the wine of about 120 communes, producing red, white and rosé.*

softer and blander; that claret at its best is the most subtle of red wines, at its worst sharp and acid; burgundy at its best rounded and fruity, at its worst heavy and unctuous.

Writers sum up the difference by recommending claret with plain roasts and grills, burgundy with game and rich stews. This is hair-splitting. Whenever you can drink burgundy, you can drink claret, and vice versa: your own taste is the only guide, and professional wine-tasters much more experienced than you or I have mistaken the one for the other before now, and will do so again.

What is more useful to remember, in my opinion, is that the wines of the Rhône, of which Châteauneuf du Pape is the most famous example, are 'bigger', more full-bodied, than either claret or burgundy, and go especially well with really rich meat dishes. So do such Italian reds as Chianti and the less frequently encountered Barolo, from northern Italy. The same is true of the red wines of North Africa – Morocco, Tunisia and Algeria, where a lot of money and a lot of French and Italian skill and experience has been put into post-war vineyards and modern wine-making plants.

The deep red wine of Châteauneuf du Pape, from the Rhône area, has one of the highest minimum strengths of any French wine (12.5% alcohol). The system of Appellations Contrôlées was initiated by its most famous grower, Baron Le Roy, in the 1920s.

30

Some good, hearty red wines come from Australia, and some delicate ones from Chile, and this is where the old comparison comes in useful. To people who know claret and burgundy better than they know Australian and Chilean reds, it is at any rate a rough guide to be told that many Australian red wines are more like burgundies, the Chileans usually more like clarets.

Red wines that are much lighter in style than those I have mentioned include Valpolicella and Bardolino, from the Italian Lakes. They are very good with the plainest of dishes and with cold meats, and are usually served cool, rather than at room temperature. The same is true of young Beaujolais (some Beaujolais is made deliberately to be drunk at not more than about a year old), a soft, fresh, fruity wine that one seems to be able to pour down in bigger gulps than most.

A basketful of the Pinot Noir grapes of Burgundy, with the fine wine they produce. Burgundy is the northernmost area in the world to produce red wine.

But here, as with every other wine-drinking convention I have mentioned, there need be no hard and fast rules. Certainly, most people in this country find that red wine with any age or body seems to be at its best at roughly the temperature of the room in which it is drunk – all you have to do is to put the bottle in the room for a couple of hours beforehand. But the French, who make the stuff, drink it much cooler: it is a matter of taste, and taste over the years becomes national custom. For that matter, a very famous French wine-lover once said that the French drink their wines too young, the English too old.

He was talking about the very finest wines, of course, and for our day-to-day drinking we can assume that when a wine is on sale it is ready for drinking. (There is more about how and when and whether to age your wine in the last chapter of this book.)

It has always seemed to me that red wine has an especial affinity with cheese. This is not to say that I have not often enjoyed a sharp or a flowery white with a rich cream cheese – the one as a contrast, the other more as a complement. But it seems more natural to choose a red, and I would go almost so far as to say that any red wine will go with any cheese. Best of all, however, is to marry full-flavoured cheese and wine (as it might be Châteauneuf du Pape and Stilton) and lighter cheese with lighter wine (claret or Valpolicella with a Caerphilly).

By all means offer both red and white at a wine-and-cheese party, but I would bet that more red will be drunk than white. The French serve the cheese before the pudding or the fruit at the end of a meal. This is so that they can go on drinking with the cheese the wine that has accompanied the main course, which is more likely to have been red than white, before going on to perhaps a mouthful of sweet wine with the pudding or fruit.

Rosé Wines with Meals

I DON'T KNOW WHY WE DON'T SIMPLY CALL THEM 'PINK'. JUST AS eating-houses over the years have become restaurants, coffee-shops cafés, and bills of fare menus, so a pink wine is rosé.

Some people affect to look down their noses at rosés: they are wines of compromise; there are no great vintage years, because they are drunk young; they are drunk young because, being taken off the skins of the grapes very quickly after pressing, they have not the tannin to give them staying power for ageing; there are no great château names because virtually all rosé wines come from co-operative wineries. All of which is wine-snob nonsense. We don't always want subtle, ten-year-old clarets, or elegant, beautifully 'balanced', white wines from single vineyards with famous names.

We don't always want the *classic* in wines any more than we do in music – there is room in life for Gilbert and Sullivan as well as for Mozart. Rosé wine looks pretty, which is a virtue in itself and, drunk young and cool, goes well with cold salmon and salads at a summer picnic, or with cold beef and potatoes in their jackets at a light supper. For picnics, incidentally, which are not in any case occasions for fine wines, rosé wines are especially suitable. Being bumped about in a car does them no harm, and they can be (indeed, must be) kept cool by taking them straight out of the fridge into insulated bags, with one of those freezer sachets inside.

The 'prickly' or, as it were, semi-sparkling Portuguese pinks acquire their slight refreshing fizziness by allowing the last stages of fermentation to complete themselves in bottle. Many wine-merchants have wines of this type, some slightly drier than others. They are not usually so cheap as the still, pink wines of France because they have to be imported in bottles, not in casks to be bottled here, in order to preserve the prickle.

Tavel is the best-known and, usually, the most expensive rosé. It comes from the southern reaches of the Rhône, where the Provençal sun packs a great deal of flavour and alcoholic strength into a wine that looks deceptively light. (Alcohol comes, not from the skins or the pips of grapes, but from the sugar. Many a white or a rosé wine is stronger in alcohol than many a red.)

There are cheaper and lighter rosés than Tavel – from Spain, Portugal and Italy – but possibly the most attractive, in colour and in their fruity style, are those of the Loire and especially of Anjou. The Cabernet d'Anjou, named

33

Vila Mateus in Portugal, home of a popular rosé wine; not all wines come from homes as distinguished as this!

after the grape it is made from, has rather more character than a simple rosé d'Anjou, made of a more prolific but less fine grape variety.

While I would always recommend (and I do so again, in a later chapter) buying the best red and white wines you can afford, which nearly always means the most expensive, I suggest that the cheapest rosé you find drinkable is good enough.

Except, that is, pink champagne. Curiously enough, this is the one rosé wine that is always called 'pink'. Now this is a wine that seems to have gone completely out of fashion. The two arguments against it are that (the purists would say) it is not a *classic* champagne, which the good Lord meant to be a white wine – though it is a blend of the juice of white grapes and the juice of black, taken immediately off the skins – and that it carries with it overtones of Victorian chorus-girl frivolity. The fact is, however, that feminine though it looks, pink champagne tends to be drier than the traditional white. It is made either by adding a little of the still red wine of the region to what would otherwise be a wine of the classic gold, or else by leaving the juice on the skins of black grapes for longer than usual. In either case, there is more of the tannin and other astringent properties that come from the skins and so, unless specially sweetened, it will be drier in style than conventional champagne, and rather fuller-bodied.

All the same, it is a spendid aperitif for a Sunday summer morning in the garden and, although I don't share the liking of the champagne-makers themselves for sparkling wine with food, it turns a picnic into a great occasion. There is more to wine than taste in the mouth. There is pleasure to the eye, and few wine-glasses so please the eye as one that looks a very pretty pink and sparkles at you.

Wines for After Dinner

SWEET WINES, LIKE SWEET DISHES, COME AT THE END OF A MEAL. THERE is, or has been, a nonsensical, half-educated snobbery about sweet wines, and I have heard red-faced, bottle-nosed, white-whiskered old men fulminating against sweet wine as a 'ladies' drink' when so full of port themselves that it seemed almost to suffuse their eyeballs. And what is port but a sweet wine?

There are two main sorts of sweet wine, the fortified – of which port is the finest example – usually drunk with cheese or nuts at the very end of the meal, or after it; and the naturally sweet wine, such as Sauternes or the sweet hocks, more usually drunk with the end-of-dinner fresh fruit or sweet pudding. The latter were discussed in the previous chapter on white wines.

It was in the early eighteenth century that port became the Englishman's traditional after-dinner drink. The Stuarts had fled to France, and their Jacobite sympathisers drank to 'the king over the water' in the wine of his country of exile – claret. War with France had led to wines from England's oldest ally, Portugal, being given a duty preference. Soon sturdy English squires were showing their loyalty to the Hanoverian line by drinking King George's health in the luscious port wine shipped from Oporto. Even now,

ABOVE *Fine old port in one of the wine-lodges of Vila Nova de Gaia, across the Douro from Oporto, where the wine matures before being shipped.*

LEFT *Port 'in the wood', waiting to be shipped. Vintage port spends only two years in cask, before being bottled: ruby may have about as much, but tawny a good deal more – the finest old tawnies from ten to as much as forty years.*

Gathering the grapes in Madeira, the wine of which achieves its characteristic caramelly taste by being baked for months in stoves at 120°F or more – a process unique to this wine and this island.

Queen Elizabeth II's health is drunk in port, because she is a Hanoverian.

There are four main sorts of port. Many consider vintage port the greatest of them all – a miraculous paradoxical mixture of strength and delicacy, sweetness and flavour. It is the product of one particularly great year (there wasn't, for instance, a vintage 'declared' between 1970 and 1975) aged for two years in the cask and anything from ten or twelve to twenty or more years in the bottle. The 1955 vintage ports are now said to be at their best, and the 1960 vintage just becoming drinkable. It is expensive, therefore, because of the many years that capital has been tied up in it.

As it ages in the bottle, vintage port creates a heavy 'crust' or deposit, so that it needs resting after every move; it needs the protective wax over the cork carefully chipped away so as not to disturb the contents of the bottle; and it needs careful decanting. It really requires either a dedicated host, or a butler.

There is an easier alternative: 'late-bottled' port is also of a vintage, but has been kept longer in the cask, where it leaves its deposit, so that it can be bottled 'bright' and needs no decanting. Cheaper and easier and, for all except vintage-port devotees, much the same sort of thing.

The other two main types of port are ruby and tawny. Ruby is the youngest port and, therefore, the cheapest – capital has been tied up in it for the shortest time. It is rich and full and so an excellent wine for everyday, after-dinner drinking, especially as it keeps its character long after the bottle has been opened, and so is economical in use.

Tawny port has aged in wood for longer (and is therefore rather dearer) to a lighter colour and a drier finish, though it is still a sweet, dessert wine. Many experts prefer an old tawny even to a vintage port for drinking with walnuts, cheese or a Cox's Orange Pippin after dinner – not, though, with tobacco, which kills the fragrance and the flavour of port.

For those who *must* smoke after dinner, I suggest an old brown or a cream dessert sherry. It is sturdy enough to stand up to clouds of cigar or cigarette smoke floating over the dinner-table, and also to remain in good heart for days after the bottle has been opened.

There are similar virtues in madeira, from the island of that name, which is rich with a caramelly flavour one either likes very much or not at all. The Bual and Malmsey types are sweeter than Sercial and Verdelho, and more suitable, therefore, for after-dinner drinking.

Underrated, and therefore underpriced, as a dessert wine is the Spanish Malaga. It is a sweet, golden or deep-gold wine with the intense flavour of the muscatel grape it is made from, a sort of poor-man's port in its satisfyingly rich after-dinner flavour, though the taste is very different.

Like madeira, Marsala, from Sicily, is an island wine and, also like madeira, it is rich and strong. Apart from being a dessert wine in its own right, it is the wine which, mixed with egg-yolk, becomes the famous Italian pudding, *zabaglione*, which Italian brides (I am told) give to Italian bridegrooms on their honeymoons. I can't think why. . . .

Sparklers, Mulls and Mixes

THE MOST FESTIVE WINES ARE THOSE THAT SPARKLE, AND THE MOST famous of the festive wines is champagne. It is with champagne that we launch – or used to launch – dreadnoughts and debutantes; champagne floats marriages and facilitates (I am told) seductions; champagne wets the baby's head and, as I have already suggested in the chapter on before-dinner drinks, whets the jaded appetite.

But all that glisters is not gold, and all that sparkles is not champagne. A celebrated court case settled that once and for all, when the judge ruled that the shippers of a sparkling wine from Spain must not advertise or label it as 'Spanish champagne'. 'Champagne' is a word that can only be used of a certain specified type of wine, made from certain specified types of grape, in a certain specified way (the *méthode champenoise*), in a specific part of France – this part of France and the *méthode champenoise* are described in a later chapter.

Fair enough, but this does not mean that other sparkling wines may not be good of their kind. Some are made by the *méthode champenoise* itself. This is basically the bringing about of a second fermentation in the bottle, and it is this which produces the bubbles. Among these are some light, yet fruity, sparkling wines from the Loire – sparkling Vouvray and sparkling Saumur.

Some are made by inducing the secondary fermentation in big tanks and then bottling under pressure. Most sparkling German wines, called *sekt* by

The right way to open a champagne bottle – 'easing' the cork out gently.

the Germans, are produced in this way, and very good they can be too. The sparkling hocks, or Rhine wines, are usually fuller in character than the more delicate sparkling Moselles.

There is no doubt that dry sparkling wines make admirable aperitifs and are excellent for parties, where they often turn out to be cheaper than mixed drinks based on gin, vodka or whisky. The sweet varieties are splendid for young people's parties.

Sparkling wines can also be enjoyed with food, and many people, especially those of the Champagne region itself, maintain that champagne is the one wine that can be drunk throughout a meal – with fish, meat, cheese, fruit, the lot. Others find this too much of a good thing. However, champagne is the perfect accompaniment for oysters (for those who can afford both at once). Also the sweet varieties, such as Italian Asti Spumante, which is fragrant with the scent of the muscatel grape it is made from, go beautifully with fruit salads and the like. The sparkle and the coolness (all sparkling wines *must* be served cool) prevent the sweetness from cloying.

Champagne, and the other dry sparklers, are also marvellous mixers. Two parts of dry fizz with one part ice-cold orange juice is called *champagne-orange* in France, and Buck's Fizz in Britain and America. In Italy alone, I think, dry sparklers are mixed with liquidised peaches and called a *Bellini*. Half-and-half with Guinness, champagne becomes Black Velvet. (Black Velveteen, say the Guinness people, if you use any other sparkler or any other stout.) And it was the shipper of one of the most famous brands of champagne who told me that on a really scorching summer's day the best of all refreshers is a glass of ice-cold champagne with a bruised sprig of mint in it.

Incidentally, before we leave sparklers, there are spring-loaded stoppers that enable you to keep the sparkle in a bottle that's been opened so that it can be put back into the fridge for another day.

We have not said a final goodbye to sparklers though, because I would now like to talk about wine cups, which are cooled mixes, and many of them

40

include sparklers. One of the various kinds of claret cup, perfect for a warm summer evening, consists of equal quantities of claret, or any lightish red wine, and any dry sparkler. Add to every two bottles of this basic mix, one glass of Grand Marnier or any similar orange liqueur (you can buy them economically in miniature one-tot bottles); the zest of a lemon – that is the thinnest outer rind – and soft sugar to taste. Chill this mixture in the refrigerator, not by adding melting ice, and you have a cup that is no weaker than any table wine and thus stimulates as well as refreshes.

A cheaper and milder cool cup is the Spanish *sangria*, of which there are many versions, some ready-mixed in bottles, and very good. To make one of your own, you need a bottle of red wine, about a quarter as much soda-water, soft sugar to taste (a heaped egg-cup is usually about right), half a lemon, a couple of sliced oranges, and some or all of the following – a pear, a peach and a slice of melon, all diced and mixed. Serve *sangria* very cold, with a big pinch of cinnamon stirred in at the last minute. Brandy can be added according to taste and the purpose of the party.

There is no end to recipes for cups. Experiment can carry the enthusiast into realms of fantasy and eventual speechlessness. . . .

A party spread, with wine and spirit mixes – whisky and soda, vermouth with ice. On the right the best appetizer of all – cool white wine.

The Wine Regions of the World

France

ABOVE *Château Lafite-Rothschild, Pauillac, home of one of the finest Bordeaux wines.*

LEFT *Burgundy grapes on the vine. The opaque 'bloom' on the grapes attracts the yeasts which cause fermentation of the wine.*

PREVIOUS PAGES *A vineyard in Burgundy, one of the world's most famous wine-growing areas.*

Champagne

IT IS A QUIET, GENTLE COUNTRYSIDE THAT PRODUCES THE WORLD'S liveliest and most lighthearted wine. The Champagne region of France is a landscape of smoothly rounded chalk downs, woodlands, vineyards and a placidly flowing river. The skies are as often grey as blue, and the climate, like the landscape, is much the same as that of southern England. It is France's northernmost wine-growing area and, except for the German Moselle, the most northerly important wine-growing region in the world.

In such a cool climate as this, grape juice ferments slowly. Fermentation is often not complete when the chill of winter comes, preventing all the grape-sugar from transforming into alcohol. So with the spring there is a tendency to create a secondary, or resumed, fermentation. The champagne method of making sparkling wine is to encourage this tendency and to induce a full secondary fermentation during the spring after the vintage.

The *méthode champenoise*, from beginning to end, is long, complicated and expensive and so would be a detailed account of it in these pages. Briefly, though, after the first, incomplete, fermentation, cultivated grape-yeasts are added, in the spring, to the young wine, along with sugar, which the yeasts convert into alcohol and into the carbonic gas that gives the wine its bubble so long as it is imprisoned in a bottle, which it is in a matter of hours.

French law imposes many restrictions on growers and wine-makers if their product is to be called 'champagne': the vines must be of a certain kind, pruned in a certain way, grown in this place and not that, the juice of their grapes fermented for a second time in the bottle, not in tanks, or in any other way not laid down by law. Yet the result is not a standardised product. The various great champagne firms each have their own house style. For instance, when the sediment has been got rid of at the end of maturing, the tiny space left in the bottle is filled by a process called 'liqueuring'. A spoonful or so of old champagne, in which a little sugar has been dissolved, is added in order to take the merest edge off what is, by nature, an austerely dry wine. Upon the amount of sugar added – which will in any case be very little – depends the relative dryness or sweetness of the wine. Thus, a *grande marque*, or leading, house such as Pommery produces a 'Dry Reserve' and a 'Carte Blanche', which is sweeter.

Then again, champagne, though a white wine, is a blend of the juice of black grapes and white. The black grapes give body and flavour, while the white grapes give finesse. The balance between the two is a matter of choice and one house will go in for a full-flavoured wine while another, equally good but different, will pride itself on lightness and delicacy, or even produce a *blanc de blancs*, from white grapes only. Bollinger and Krug, for instance, are small, old-fashioned firms that produce wines with considerable 'body': Moët and Chandon's premium brand, Dom Pérignon, is lighter in style altogether.

There are cheaper champagnes. They are also made in strict conformity with French law but, perhaps, from grapes grown in vineyards that do not enjoy the best soil or the most sunshine. Alternatively they can be made from

ABOVE *Champagne vineyards at Ay, Epernay.*

OPPOSITE *Real champagne is sparkling and clear, its bubbles and froth are fine and persistent.*

TOP *Champagne vineyards in winter.*

ABOVE *Filling a champagne press at Epernay. Champagne, though a white wine, is a blend of the juice of black grapes and white.*

the third of the three permitted pressings of the grapes, while the very finest wines use only the juice from the first pressing and perhaps part of the second. Even these lesser champagnes, however, have the sparkling gaiety that makes it the most lighthearted of party drinks, the most appetising of aperitifs.

Vintage champagne, from the grapes of one year only, is always fuller and 'bigger' than non-vintage, for the year must be a good one and the grape juice will have been richer. Non-vintage is made with at least as much care, using a blend of this year and that, as well as of black and white grapes and of this vineyard and that. The non-vintage of a good house will be beautifully balanced and more of an all-purpose wine than a vintage.

The name 'champagne' is so jealously guarded that the famous local mustard may not be labelled as being made of mustard and champagne even though it is. It has to be described as consisting of 'mustard seed with wine from the Champagne district'. For a long time, it was forbidden to export the still white wine of the region – Coteaux Champenois – lest fraudulent foreigners pumped bubbles into it and called it champagne. Now, though, it is permitted, Coteaux Champenois is elegant, dry, fruity and very expensive, naturally enough, otherwise it would be more profitable to use it for champagne. The local red wine is like a very light burgundy. The most agreeable thing about it is that it is called, from the district of its origin, Bouzy.

Burgundy

BURGUNDY IS GREAT EATING-AND-DRINKING COUNTRY. BETWEEN
Dijon and Lyons are more restaurants starred in the gastronomic guides than
in any other part of the country of similar size. The butchers and fishmongers
and cooked-meat shops offer a mouth-watering selection: Charollais beef,
black puddings, tripe sausages, and the plump, white-fleshed cockerels and
capons of Bresse; snails fattened on vine-leaves and pink ham set in parsley-
green jelly; trout and carp and pike and eels; truffles and mushrooms and
furred game and feathered game; wine sauces and spiced mustards; honey-
cakes and luscious confections of juicy blackcurrants and thick, yellow
cream.

And to accompany these, and a thousand other delicacies, the wines of the
region – red wines rivalled only by the clarets of Bordeaux and white wines
equal in renown to the finest that Germany produces. Different in style
though. For where German wines are, so to speak, feminine in their lightness
and fragrance and immediate charm, white burgundy at its best is masculine
in its firmness and more austere than the flowery wines of the Rhine and
Moselle (or, for that matter, than other white wines of France) yet with great
depth of flavour and character. For those who like white wine with meat
dishes and with fish in the richest sauces, white burgundy has the necessary
fullness not to be overwhelmed by the most savoury dish.

This, of course, is to speak of the white burgundies such as Meursault and
Montrachet. There are lighter wines, such as Chablis, that go well with the
plainer fish dishes. There are cheaper wines such as Bourgogne Aligoté,
named after its grape, which is more prolific than the classic white grapes of
the region. It is a useful and pleasant table wine, especially good as an aperitif
with a spoonful of *crème de cassis*, the sweet blackcurrant cordial of the
region, mixed into it.

But only one-sixth of the wine-production of the region is white. When
wine-lovers speak of 'burgundy', *tout court*, it is red burgundy that they refer
to and as often as not in comparison with claret, the red wine of Bordeaux.
Burgundy is regarded as the fuller, fruitier wine of the two, but the
differences are often exaggerated if only because the similarities between
claret and burgundy are so great.

Burgundy is not to be regarded as a wine so rich and full that it would be
port if it could. It can be very light and uncloying, though at its most
characteristic it is softer and rounder than a typical claret, with a hint more of
a grapey sweetness; and it matures earlier. Except for the very finest
burgundies, such as Chambertin and Richebourg and Romanée, five years or
so is quite a decent age for a burgundy, certainly for those with simply a
district name such as Beaune, Volnay or Pommard. It is perhaps at its best
with the classic dish of its own region – *bœuf bourguignonne*, which is beef
stewed in burgundy – for wine always goes well with a dish cooked in itself.

We must not leave Burgundy, though, without mention of the region
sometimes referred to as South Burgundy, but better known as the
Beaujolais, whence comes one of the world's most justly popular wines.

Beaujolais vineyards at Juliénas in Burgundy.

Some Beaujolais is made to mature and to be drunk like burgundy or claret, but most of it is made to be drunk young and cellar-cool. A wine meant to be gulped rather than sipped and mouth-filling in its fruitness, it is an especially good companion to the softer, runnier French cheeses such as Brie and Camembert.

But all red wines go well with cheese, and burgundy itself is a handsome companion to the hard or crumbly English cheeses such as Cheddar and Cheshire, Lancashire and Leicester and Wensleydale. Even to Stilton, though I can understand those who insist that port is none too full a wine for so majestic a cheese.

Bordeaux

JUST AS BURGUNDY IS SO FAMOUS FOR ITS COOKING AS TO BE CALLED THE belly of France, so the Bordeaux region must be regarded as France's wine-cellar. Five hundred square miles of vineyards, in the south-western corner of the country, that has Bordeaux as its centre and its capital, produce on average one-tenth of all the wines of France. No place in the world produces so much fine wine, from the luscious white dessert wines of Sauternes to the great reds of St Emilion and the Médoc.

First, the white wines. Around Bordeaux itself, and the south-eastern area along the left bank of the River Garonne, is the Graves, where both reds and whites are grown. The whites, even when dry, have a hint of fruit and a good deal of body. The locals drink them with the splendid oysters of nearby Arcachon.

To the south is the prettily wooded Sauternais, a region of light sweet white wines, sold simply as 'Sauternes' or 'Barsac'. Sauternais also produces great, lusciously rich, dessert wines sold under their château names, such as Coutet and the famous Yquem itself. These are made from overripe grapes that have been attacked by the fungus 'noble rot', which causes the water content to evaporate so that the grapes shrivel on the vine like sultanas, leaving a concentrate of sugar and flavour. The resulting golden wine is almost oily in its richness, with a remarkably intense fragrance and sweetness. The people who grow these great wines can drink them with the *pâté de foie gras* of the district, on the principle that rich food calls for a rich wine. I find the combination cloying, but much enjoy a small glass after a meal as a sort of liquid dessert.

The district's other good white wines are overshadowed by the dry Graves and the sweet Sauternes. In the same way, the many sound reds of both sides of the river are overshadowed by the great clarets of the Médoc, Pomerol and St Emilion. Many wine-lovers consider that from these regions come the noblest red wines of all. At any rate, only the greatest burgundies can really be compared with them.

The most famous clarets of all are those of the Médoc, especially the sixty or so 'classified' wines, each with a château name – it might be Lafite or Mouton, Margaux or Latour. But these constitute a sort of aristocracy of clarets, among a thousand or more named wines, many of them nature's

Bottles of Chambertin from Burgundy.

LEFT *The vineyards of Entre Deux Mers in the Bordeaux region.*

ABOVE *Inspecting the grapes for 'noble rot' at Château d'Yquem.*

ABOVE *Château Lafite is often considered the supreme wine of the Pauillac region.*

TOP *Three examples of artistic label-design for Mouton Rothschild bottles. Every year Baron Philippe de Rothschild commissions a famous artist to decorate the labels for his bottles.*

gentlemen at least. Between all of them there is a sort of family resemblance, with the usual minor differences that exist between members of the same family.

The wines of Pomerol and St Emilion, for instance, on the other side of Bordeaux, are softer and fruitier, and are closer to burgundy, than the more reserved Médocs. They are quicker to mature, too, which makes most of them cheaper, because money has to be tied up a shorter time before they are ready to drink.

It is pleasant to take an aperitif of dry white Graves in Libourne, the busy little trading centre of St Emilion and Pomerol, and then drive to the picturesque walled town of St Emilion itself. Here one can take lunch on the terrace, enjoying the sweeping view of vineyards, with a claret to accompany the *entrecôte Bordelaise*, which is steak in red wine and shallots, and a glass of Sauternes afterwards with the macaroons that are the little town's speciality. This is a happy hunting ground for delicious things to eat, and for good wine to go with them.

The Loire

FRANCE'S LONGEST RIVER, THE LOIRE, FLOWS THROUGH SOME OF France's loveliest countryside. The princes and noblemen of the French High Renaissance built their châteaux on its banks – settings now for *son et lumière*

54

displays on summer evenings – because of the glowing skies, the lush countryside, and the benign, temperate climate. Also because of the game. This was, and still is to a lesser extent, country that resounds to the bay of the hounds and the sound of the horn. And, not least, because of the grape and other fruit, for this is a land both of orchards and of vineyards. In Angers a plaque commemorates the raising in 1849–50 of that fistful of fragrance and of flavour, the Comice pear. Three centuries before that, the writer and laureate of good living, François Rabelais, roared out his pride in the fact that the sleepy little country town of La Chartre, on a tributary of the Loire near where he was born, was full of wine-merchants and boasted of at least twenty-seven tavern-keepers. Not bad, for a place that even to this day numbers fewer than two thousand men, women and children.

As in Rabelais's day, the Loire is still, as it were, a river of wine. It links the Sancerre and Pouilly-Fumé (not to be confused with Pouilly-Fuissé) produced on its upper reaches, which border Burgundy, with the Muscadet produced on the Atlantic coast and fit companion for that same seaboard's succulent oysters.

These wines are white, as are most of the wines of the Loire. Many of them (but not the Muscadet) are made from the Sauvignon grape which, in this temperate climate, makes a clean, light wine with enough fruit to give fragrance and flavour, enough acidity to give a refreshing crispness. The wines of Vouvray, though, derive from the Chénin Blanc grape, and are softer and sweeter. Similarly, sparkling Vouvray is softer and sweeter than champagne, though it is made in the same way. The grape and the soil make the difference.

Saumur, elegant riverside city of horses and horsemen, home of the French army's riding academy and of the Cadre Noir (France's equivalent of Vienna's Spanish Riding School), produces a rosé wine which is rather drier than those of the surrounding district of Anjou. The sparkler of this city is rather more full-bodied than those of Vouvray because it has more of the juice of black grapes blended with the white.

Near here, too, are sweet white wines of which the Quarts de Chaume are the best known. They are made like the great Sauternes of Bordeaux and, at their best, similarly full in flavour and high in alcohol, though they always seem fresher and less cloying than such grander rivals, because of their underlying acidity.

And so to the mouth of the river and its famous wine, Muscadet. This has become the white equivalent of Beaujolais. It is a drinking-man's wine, to be quaffed, not sipped, and a basic wine for meals at home, or to take by the glass in a bar, a café, or in modest restaurants. The best Muscadets, and the most, come from the banks of the tributary River Sèvre, have the legal *appellation* Sèvre et Maine, and are made from the grape the wine is named after. There is a drier, less distinguished wine of the region, made from the Gros Plant grape. As Muscadet has become more expensive so Gros Plant has become more widely planted, and better known.

Both wines should be drunk well chilled, and go splendidly with fish, as well they should in this paradise for fish-eaters. Like Beaujolais, they are drunk young and fresh. There is something of a vogue for Muscadet-sur-lie, which is bottled in the early spring after the vintage, direct from the wood it

55

ENGLISH CHANNEL

Dunkirk
Calais
Dieppe
Le Havre
Cherbourg
Seine
Orléans
Loire
ANJOU   TOURAINE
MUSCADET   Tours
Saumur
Nantes   THE LOIRE
Loudun
Châtellerault
Poitiers

ATLANTIC OCEAN

CHARENTE
COGNAC
Cognac   Limoges

Gironde
Bordeaux
BORDEAUX   Bergerac
Dordogne

Garonne   Cahors

Toulouse

P Y R E N E E S

MÉDOC
Gironde
BLAYAIS
St Estèphe
Pauillac
St Julien   Blaye   BOURGEAIS
HAUT MÉDOC   FRONSAC
Margaux   • Bourg   NÉAC
Néac   POMEROL
Fronsac   • Pomerol
Vayres   Libourne   ST ÉMILION
Dordogne
BORDEAUX   VAYRES
Bordeaux   ENTRE-DEUX-MERS
GRAVES   CÔTES DE BORDEAUX
Barsac   • St Macaire
Garonne
SAUTERNES
Isle

Bordeaux Rouge
APPELLATION BORDEAUX CONTROLÉE

Bordeaux Blanc
APPELLATION BORDEAUX CONTROLÉE

PRODUCE OF FRANCE   PRODUCE OF FRANCE
70cl   70cl

GRANTS OF ST JAMES'S
Muscadet
APPELLATION CONTROLÉE
70cl

Main wine-producing areas

Secondary wine-producing areas

• Reims

Marne

CHAMPAGNE

• Strasbourg

VOSGES

ALSACE

Saône

Dijon •

• Besançon

JURA

• Beaune

JURA

BURGUNDY

• Mâcon

BEAUJOLAIS

Rhône

• Lyon

SAVOY

Grenoble •

ALPS

SSIF
ENTRAL

THE RHÔNE

• Nice

Nîmes •

PROVENCE

Montpellier •

• Marseille

LANGUEDOC-
ROUSSILLON

cassone

MEDITERRANEAN SEA

• Perpignan

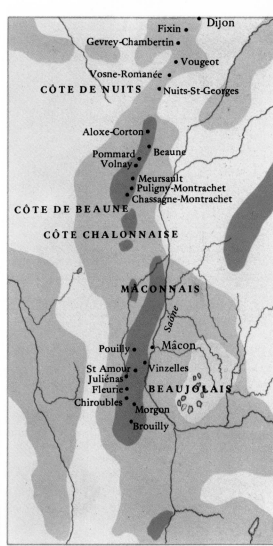

Dijon •
Fixin •
Gevrey-Chambertin •
• Vougeot
Vosne-Romanée •
CÔTE DE NUITS
• Nuits-St-Georges

Aloxe-Corton •
Pommard •
• Beaune
Volnay •
Meursault •
Puligny-Montrachet •
Chassagne-Montrachet
CÔTE DE BEAUNE
CÔTE CHALONNAISE

MÂCONNAIS

Saône

Pouilly •
• Mâcon
St Amour •
• Vinzelles
Juliénas •
Fleurie •
BEAUJOLAIS
Chiroubles •
• Morgon
• Brouilly

Vintage time in the Loire valley.

has fermented in, and thus straight from the *lie* (or sediment) instead of having previously been 'racked' from one cask to another, to leave the sediment behind. This wine seems to gain some quality of fruitiness and fullness from contact with the *lie*.

What, though, of the reds of the region? They are but two, and they come from small towns that straddle the middle of the river, not far from Tours – Chinon and Bourgueil. They are made from the Cabernet Franc grape of St Emilion, and they bear a family resemblance to St Emilion's clarets. But they are lighter, and they show well when served cool, as though they were rosé wines. They are never better than by the banks of the great river, with a picnic of cold meats (*charcuterie*), before an evening of *son et lumière* at one of the nearby châteaux.

Alsace, Jura and Savoy

ALSACE IS AS PECULIAR AND HIGHLY INDIVIDUAL A PART OF FRANCE and as different from the rest of the country as Wales, say, is from the rest of the United Kingdom, or the Basque country from the rest of Spain. For one thing, it looks not French but German. Its picture-postcard villages, with their overhanging half-timbered gables and their storks' nests, might well be Disney film sets for Grimm brothers' fairy tales.

Alsatian vineyards with high-trained vines link picturesque half-timbered villages between the Vosges mountains and the Rhine.

Despite this, Alsace does not *feel* German, and the Alsatian considers himself very much a Frenchman, even if a rather special kind of Frenchman. However, he does speak German or, at any rate, a German dialect, and the family names and many of the forenames of the district are German. Alsace eats German, too. Its cuisine is based upon the goose, its fat and its liver; on pork and on sausages; on red cabbage and white cabbage, fresh cabbage and sauerkraut.

As with the food, so with the wine. The wines of Alsace, grown on the slopes of the Vosges, a little to the west of the Rhine, are recognisably related to the German wines of the Rhine itself and of its tributaries. Much more akin to them, indeed, than to anything grown in the rest of France. Understandably so: they are made from grapes grown in the same sort of soil, and under the same sort of climatic conditions. But chiefly it is the grapes themselves. The finest wines of Alsace, like those of Germany, are made from the Riesling grape, especially, and also from the Sylvaner and the Gewürztraminer. (Note, incidentally, that these are all white-wine grapes. The reds and the rosés of Alsace are even less frequent and less distinguished than those of Germany.)

Where they do differ from those of Germany it is a matter not of style – the style is similar – but in dryness. Generally speaking, the typical Alsatian Riesling, Sylvaner or Gewürztraminer is similar to, but drier than, its German counterpart. The reason is that the Alsatian growers ferment their wines fully, so that all the grape-sugar is converted into alcohol, whereas the Germans like to retain some unfermented juice, to preserve a little softness and sweetness. Another difference between the wines of Alsace and those of both France and Germany is that each Alsatian wine is named after its grape, not after the place it is grown. Thus, one looks for an Alsatian Riesling or an Alsatian Sylvaner, not for a Schloss Johannisberg or a Château d'Yquem.

The Riesling, at its best, has a balance of fruitiness and acidity that is both refreshing and satisfying, with a delicacy of fragrance and flavour that makes the Gewürztraminer, to some tastes at least, too obvious in its appeal. This wine, though, for all its opulent bouquet – I have known an opened bottle and glassful to scent a whole room – and its strength of flavour, is quite dry at the finish, so that it goes supremely well, and better than the more delicate Riesling, with the most savoury dishes and richest sauces. I have even known it recommended with the lightly curried French dishes *à l'Indienne*. The Alsatians themselves like to drink it with their famous truffled Strasbourg *pâté de foie gras*, on the principle that rich food calls for rich wine. The Sylvaner is softer than the Riesling, with less acidity, but refreshing in spite of

Riquewihr, one of the most picturesque little towns of Alsace, is French in feeling, but German-speaking. It is one of the best placed areas of Alsace, with south-facing slopes standing out from the Vosges.

its blandness, easy to drink and usually very good value for money – an excellent aperitif wine.

Cheaper still, of course, are the wines made in Alsace from less distinguished grapes, or from blends of those that I have named with grapes of commoner stock. In Alsace itself, these are usually labelled simply as 'Vin d'Alsace', or as 'Zwicker' or (higher up the social scale) as 'Edelzwicker'. Outside their native country, they are more frequently found under brand names – 'Flambeau d'Alsace', 'Chevalier d'Alsace' and the like.

All the wines of the region must be made according to the requirements of the French wine law, which the Alsatians adhere to strictly, and their general level is high. Indeed, I cannot recall having drunk a badly made Alsatian wine. Even the most modest, and at their worst they can be very slight, always have a touch of the true Alsatian style: crisply refreshing, with a whisper of the grape they come from, so that the tall, tapering green bottle always seems to hold the promise of at least a light fragrance to the nose and a pretty hint of freshness and fruit in the mouth.

South of Alsace, facing not Germany but Switzerland, lie the Jura and Savoy, two beautiful mountain regions. The Jura is noted for its pink wines, which in those parts are called not rosé, but *gris*; for a sparkling wine called *vin fou* (mad wine); and for *vin jaune* which is a strong, dry, nutty aperitif wine, rather like sherry. Better known is the sparkling wine of Savoy, Seyssel. It is made in the same way as champagne, and is a good alternative. Savoy is also known for its Chambéry vermouth, drier than most other French vermouths, and especially suitable for dry Martinis. It gives flavour and fragrance without loss of dryness, so there is no need to overdo the gin.

The Rhône and the South

THE WINES OF THE RHÔNE ARE GROWN NO FARTHER SOUTH THAN the clarets of Bordeaux, and yet they are much more southern in character – fuller in flavour and usually stronger in alcohol. This is because, whereas the Bordeaux climate is tempered by Atlantic breezes, the Rhône valley, running north to south, forms a funnel for the hot south winds of the Mediterranean. These, together with the heat of the southern sun reflected from the stones of this arid region, ripen grapes until they are packed with sugar, their skins full of colour, flavour and the tannin that gives staying-power to the wine.

There are four main wine-growing regions in the Rhône valley. Beginning at the north with the Côte Rôtie (the roasted hillside), the red wines of this district, though fuller in the ways I have indicated than those of Burgundy and Bordeaux, are the lightest of the Rhônes. This is partly because they come from the northernmost part of this basically southern region; partly because the best vineyards are five hundred feet or so above sea-level; partly because a small amount of the white Viognier grape is added to the black Syrah in their making. There are famous restaurants in the little towns of this district, and at them are to be enjoyed, as well as the best local reds, the dry, flavoury white wines of Condrieu. They are, in fact, a deep

60

golden colour and the most renowned, and therefore the most expensive, of them is Château Grillet.

Downstream, the great rock of Hermitage towers over the Rhône like a riverside Gibraltar, marking the second of our Rhône regions. From its slopes comes the big, hearty red wine of the same name, once as well known in Britain as claret. Hermitage is coming into its own again. Although it is usually sold quite young, so that it may be fairly cheap and under-priced for its quality, it will usually repay a few months' bottle-age after purchase. Crozes-Hermitage is nearly as good though not quite – it comes from slopes less sunny. The whites of the region are strong in flavour as whites go.

A few miles downstream, by way of the third region of the Rhône, whence come two estimable sparkling wines – Saint Péray (full-bodied) and Clairette de Die (lighter and a shade sweeter) – and we are in the country of the great Châteauneuf du Pape itself. The wine is so called because it comes

The hillsides of Tain, overlooking the valley of the Rhône, covered by vineyards whence comes the full-flavoured wine of Hermitage. Wine has been grown here since Roman times.

from around the village where Pope John XII, having already established himself at Avignon, built his *château neuf* as a summer residence. While never so delicate as the best burgundies or clarets, it is not only stronger in body and in alcohol but has a magnificent bouquet. It is a splendid accompaniment to the richest stews, dishes of game and vociferous cheeses. Gigondas is a similar wine, though less well known.

Tavel, another wine of the district, has an even higher rank among rosés than Châteauneuf has among reds. It is full in flavour and in alcoholic strength and, though not to be trifled with as we do with some similarly pretty wines, its strength makes it keep well. So it is an ideal wine to have as a standby. A few bottles in the house will serve for winter buffet suppers as well as for the summer picnics, at which it looks so charming.

Last of our Rhône wines, and appropriately so because it is an end-of-the-meal wine, is Beaumes de Venise, made from the muscat grape, only lightly luscious, and superb with fruit.

Strictly speaking, Châteauneuf du Pape and Tavel are in Provence, but we regard their wines as Rhône wines because of their high quality. It is to their south and east that the vast vineyards of France's deep south grow high-yielding vines producing more common wines. Riviera restaurateurs sell them to the sun-worshipping holiday-makers from the north. Nowadays the growers of the region are taking more trouble with their wines than they used to. For instance, the white wine from Cassis, a picturesque little harbour-town near Marseilles (not to be confused with *liqueur de cassis*, which is the blackcurrant cordial of Dijon), goes well with the rich fish dishes of the coast. The reds of Bandol complement perfectly the even richer stews. The rosés of this holiday country are holiday wines.

From the western banks of the lower Rhône to the foothills of the eastern Pyrenees, Languedoc and Roussillon are a sea of vines. This hot, arid, wildly beautiful, brigandish country is France's most productive and least distinguished wine-growing area. Hot climates generally produce strong, coarse wines, but not if low-grade vines are cultivated for the sake of heavy yields. The wines of this area are often so weak in style and in alcohol that they have to be given guts by blending them with wines from North Africa, Spain, Portugal or Italy. Still, there are attempts to raise some of the region's wines to higher standards so as to profit from the overseas demand for sound French wines cheaper than the classics. Minervois and Corbières are names that have become known in Britain since 1973, and may well become better known still.

From this corner of France, westward to the coast and northward to Bordeaux, is a wildly diverse countryside. Just as its various districts have no common character, neither have its wines and none is especially well known abroad. There is a powerful red wine, so intensely deep in colour that it is known as the black wine of Cahors, from the banks of the Lot, south-east of Bordeaux. There is a sweetish white wine, Monbazillac, and a sweeter one, Jurançon, from near Pau. The only Basque wine that I know of as being exported is Irouléguy. It is rich in flavour and in fragrance with an interesting bitter finish and better for dinner than for lunch and for winter than for summer.

Grapes ripe and ready for picking in Provence, most prolific of France's wine-growing regions. Its best vineyards are those of the Côtes de Provence, between the Alps and the Mediterranean.

62

Germany, Switzerland and Austria

*Assmanshausen, on the Rhine, whence
comes one of the best-known of
Germany's few red wines.*

The Rhine

GERMANY'S WINE PRODUCTION IS A MERE ONE-TENTH THAT OF France, or of Italy, but it includes some of the finest white wines in the world – some of them from the banks of the Moselle, but most of them from the river's big brother, the Rhine.

Virtually all Rhine wines – about eighty-five per cent of the total production – are white. They are known in the English-speaking world as hocks, and are easily recognisable in their slender, shoulderless, amber-coloured bottles. Easily recognisable, too, is their characteristic balance of fruitiness, fragrance and a refreshing acidity – generally a little softer, a little more rounded in the mouth, than their cousins of the Moselle. However, I use the word 'cousin' deliberately, for there is a marked family resemblance, due partly to their both being cool-climate wines, and to the fact that the same grapes are grown in both regions.

Wines grown in a cool climate are usually fragrant, low in alcohol and with the same sort of acidity that one finds in fresh fruit, whereas it is body and depth that one finds in wines, particularly red wines, grown under a hotter sun.

The greatest hocks are made from the Riesling grape, as are most Moselles. Other German grapes such as the Müller-Thurgau and the Silvaner ('Sylvaner', in Alsace) make similarly fragrant and fruitily acid wines.

There are Rhineland wine-growing regions all the way from the shores of Lake Constance, where Switzerland and Germany meet, and where the Rhine rises, to Bonn, which is on the same latitude as Bournemouth, in the south of England. Most of the hocks we know, however, come from four chief regions: the Rheingau, along the north bank of the river where it turns to run east to west for about twenty miles between Mainz and Bingen; the valley of the Nahe, which runs into the Rhine at Bingen; and the two great areas stretching south from Mainz along the west bank of the Rhine all the way to the French frontier, and split into Rheinhessen and the Palatinate. Other regions to the east and the south – Franconia and Baden-Württemberg – grow interesting wines, those of Franconia drier than hocks, and bottled in squat flagons, but they are not often seen outside Germany.

The Rheingau wines are the aristocrats of hocks. As the vineyards are sheltered from the north by the Taunus mountains and face south to the sun and its reflection from the river, they produce full-flavoured, smooth wines. They have been called 'old-fashioned and romantic' and are delightful to linger over. Johannisberg is a great Rheingau name. The wines of Schloss Johannisberg itself are world-famous, and those of the slopes upon which it stands deservedly share their glory. Rüdesheim produces perhaps rather fuller and less subtle wines, but true Rheingau in style.

Geographically, the Nahe valley lies between those of the Rhine and the Moselle, and its wines at their best seem to combine the delicacy of the Moselles with the greater depth of hock. A good Schloss Bockelheimer seems to capture the very spirit of all German wines.

The best-known Rhine wine of all, Liebfraumilch, came originally

Bacharach, splendidly situated on the north bank of the Rhine, in the Rheingau, produces a typically fresh and fragrant hock.

Inside the cellars of Schloss Johannisberg, one of the Rheingau's most celebrated estates.

from Rheinhessen, which lies between Bingen and the cathedral town of Worms. The name derived from the monastery vineyards of the Liebfrauen church in Worms but is now permitted by German law to almost any Rhine wine of good quality – usually a blend from various vineyards in the region. It is a soft, bland wine with a fair amount of sweetness. Being a blend, it can be made consistent in style and quality year by year, and so it is sometimes reassuring to see the name on an unfamiliar wine-list.

The Palatinate also makes soft hocks, heavier in flavour than most. The sweeter ones are made from overripe grapes, some that have even become sultana-like on the vine (Beerenauslesen and Trockenbeerenauslesen). As luscious dessert wines they should be drunk in small glasses at the end of a meal, almost as port is, or a liqueur.

German law jealously protects the reputation of all German wines, and to carry the word Qualitätswein on its label a wine has to pass rigorous tasting tests by independent panels. At one that I was privileged to attend, an otherwise perfectly good wine, that you or I might well have enjoyed, was denied the categorisation because the panel decided that it must have come from beside a pine wood and that pine needles must have blown on to the ripening grapes more than usual.

The Moselle

THE RIVER MOSELLE RISES IN THE FRENCH VOSGES, AND FLOWS through Luxembourg and Germany to its confluence with the Rhine at Koblenz. It twists and turns through more than three hundred miles, most of them pretty; some of them, indeed, dramatically beautiful because of the steep, cliff-like banks; virtually all of them, French, Luxembourgeois and German, criss-crossed with vineyards. The German stretch and, more particularly, the forty-mile middle of the German stretch, is the northernmost wine-growing region of any size or importance. Its wines are world-famous for their subtlety and fragrance.

Compared with other German wines – Rhine wines or hocks – Moselles are lighter and more delicate, sopranos compared with contraltos, say, or tenors with baritones. This is not to say that there is not a family resemblance, too, and some overlapping of style, but German wine-lovers talk of 'the lords of the Rhine and the ladies of the Moselle'.

It is the soil and the grape that make Moselle, or Moselwein – slate soil and the Riesling grape. There is a theory that civilisation is a response to challenge, but to a challenge that *can* be met; so the world's most delicate wines are grown where the vine has to struggle for survival, but where it *can* survive. In the valley of the Moselle and its tributaries, the cool, northern climate and the poorness of the soil make a struggle necessary. But the deep valley is sheltered from the keen winds and the sharp frosts that sweep and bite the hilltops, and the slate holds moisture and reflects heat.

Although the Moselle flows generally a little east of north, its winding is such that it often flows due west or due east, so that vineyards on its right bank or its left face south and the sun. This advantage has been intensified by the river's recent canalisation, which has not only made transport easier and cheaper but increased the surface of water above each lock, and with it the reflection of warmth and light on to the vines.

The greatest wines of the region come from the middle Moselle and the valleys of two small tributaries, the Saar and the Ruwer. However, in the middle Moselle there is a another challenge to add to those presented by the cold climate and the poor soil – steepness. This, too, makes for quality: there are vineyards so nearly vertical that no machine or animal can work them and yet this, too, makes for quality. Men carry everything up and down on their backs – earth, to replace what has been washed down by the rain, fertilisers, tools, pesticides and spraying machines and, eventually, grapes. Men will not go to this trouble for run-of-the-mill results. It is the fate of the wine-growers of the Moselle to be perfectionists.

Here is one reason why Moselle wines are inescapably dear. Another is the climate. There is no such thing as a coarse or a common Moselle wine, but in a bad year with little sunshine, the wines of this northerly region, and especially those of the Saar and the Ruwer, can be thin and unsatisfying. Such wines do not reach the market as Moselle wines, but go cheaply to the sparkling-wine factories. The growers lose money and recoup by charging proportionately more for the wines of good years. And they are worth it.

In its tall green bottle, the wine itself with the merest whisper of a hint of green and gold to an otherwise water-white, a typical Moselle seems almost to flirt with one, so feminine is its fragrance and its fruity sweetness. This is balanced by a similarly fruity acidity, as in a perfect strawberry or apple or, indeed, as in the grape that it comes from.

The Germans themselves drink this kind of wine before or after, rather than during, meals and I cannot think of anything more delicious than a long, cool glass of Moselle in the garden on a summer's Sunday morning, or to talk away an evening with. But Moselle goes well, too, with fish and particularly with the more delicate fish such as trout. Those who find white burgundy too austere for shellfish can match the light steeliness of a Saar or a Ruwer wine with the sea-water saltiness of oysters. And the lightest and most digestible late-night snack I can think of would be a sandwich of the white meat of chicken and a glass of Moselle to wash it down with.

Vineyards at Bernkastel, on the Moselle, home of one of Germany's finest and most expensive Rieslings.

67

Zeltinger Riesling
MOSEL SAAR RUWER

Kron Prinz
LIEBFRAUMILCH
An excellent, slightly sweet, Rhine wine with a pleasant bouquet
Shipped and bottled by
EDWARD YOUNG & CO.
LONDON LIVERPOOL & GLASGOW

GERMANY

TAUNUS MOUNTAINS

Rhine

● Frankfurt

● Bonn

Remagen ● ● Linz

Ahr

Lahn

● Würzburg

MOSEL-
SAAR-
RUWER

● Mülheim ● Koblenz

FRANCONIA

Moselle

RHEINGAU

Main

Saale

Bernkastel ———
Neumagen ———
Piesport ———
Ruwer ———
Trier ———
Saarburg ———

Wiesbaden ●

Hochheim

● Mainz

Nierstein
Oppenheim

RHEINHESSEN

Johannisberg ———
Rüdesheim ———
Bad Kreuznach ———
Bad Münster ———
Schlossbockelheim ———

Neckar

NAHE

Mannheim ●
● Heidelberg

Nahe

Speyer ●

WÜRTTEMBERG

PALATINATE

Stuttgart ● *Dan*

● Baden-Baden

BADEN

Lake Constance

● Basel

● Zürich

NEUCHATEL

A
L
P
S

VAUD SWITZERLAND

● Lausanne

Geneva ● *Lake Geneva*

TICINO

VALAIS

Piesporter Michelsberg
MOSEL SAAR RUWER

Terraced vineyards on the banks of the river Moselle in Germany.

AUSTRIA

Vienna

Salzburg

Main wine-producing areas

Switzerland

MANY GREAT WINES ARE GROWN ON THE STEEPEST OF HILLSIDES — one has only to look at those of the Moselle — but few on high mountains. Italy's Val d'Aosta region does have some vineyards at three thousand feet above sea-level. The vineyards of Visperterminen, near Mount Zermatt, are almost four thousand feet above sea-level, the highest in Europe, and are exceptional even in Alpine Switzerland. However, most of the country's wines come from the valley of the Rhône and from the shores of Lake Geneva and Lake Neuchâtel, in the cantons of the Valais and the Vaud, all of them in French-speaking Switzerland.

The dry white Fendant, stronger than it looks or tastes, comes from the Valais, around the town of Sion. The rather bland red Dôle comes from the same district. It is made from a blend of the juice of two varieties of vine, Burgundy's Pinot Noir and the Gamay of the Beaujolais. These are the two Swiss wines best known abroad, but there are some pleasant sparklers from the shores of Lake Neuchâtel, as well as a 'partridge-eye', *oeil de perdrix*, pink.

Not a great deal of Swiss wine is exported. The Swiss drink most of what they grow, and import more, especially good red burgundy.

ABOVE *Spraying the vines against pests in the Valais region of the Bernese Oberland, Switzerland. Vines can be attacked by many pests: the cochylis moth, tiny red spiders, mildew, powdery mildew, and phylloxera.*

Austria

AUSTRIA IS AN ALPINE COUNTRY, TOO. ITS WINES, LIKE THOSE OF Switzerland, come mainly from a river valley, that of the Danube, and from a lakeside, that of the Neusiedler See.

There is very little Austrian red wine, and although many French and German white grape varieties are grown, the most Austrian of Austrian wines is made from the country's own Grüner Veltliner, which produces a dry white wine. It is spicy, like an Alsatian Gewürztraminer, and with an underlying, refreshing crispness, like the Riesling. This is the Austrian wine best known abroad. Most of it comes from the Wachau, a craggy, steep-sloped stretch of the Danube valley, only an hour's drive from Vienna. This district has some good co-operatives and a few individual producers, notably Lenz Moser, a great innovator, and Prince Metternich, whose Schloss Grafenegg is to be found on many a wine-list.

Perhaps the best place, though, to enjoy the wines of Austria is at a *heurigen*. This is one of the wine-gardens of Grinzing, the Vienna suburb, where the wine of the year is served in quarter-litre tumblers at trestle tables. You bring your own picnic food, your children and your grandma; listen to a fiddler or a concertina-player; and enjoy yourself, the music and the wine, and do not take yourself, the music or the wine, too seriously.

OPPOSITE *A vineyard in the Inn valley, eastern Switzerland. Almost every canton in Switzerland makes a little wine.*

Italy

ABOVE *Serralunga d'Alba, in Piedmont, where they grow the rich, red, Barolo wine that is one of Italy's finest.*

OPPOSITE *Vineyards at Monte Giovi, Tuscany.*

WINE IS GROWN THROUGHOUT THE LENGTH OF THAT LONG LEG OF land that is Italy, more wine than in any other country in the world. It is grown by French-speaking Italians in the Val d'Aosta, which is farther north than where the French themselves grow claret; it is grown by German-speaking Italians in the Alto Adige, which is as far north as Burgundy; and it is grown by Sicilians on the same latitude as Athens. It is grown a couple of thousand feet up the Alpine slopes of Piedmont and at sea-level on Sardinian shores and by the Adriatic. It is grown from classic French and German grapes, such as the Pinot and the Riesling, and from vines known only in Italy that date from Roman and even Etruscan times.

So there is a vast variety of Italian wines. When I wrote a book about them, a dozen years ago, I listed more than six hundred, and have learned

Vintage time in Piedmont. Piedmontese wine, strong and rich, is bottled in Burgundian-shaped bottles of brown glass.

74

VAL
D'AOSTA

Lake
Como

ALTO-ADIGE
• Trento

Turin •

• Milan

VENETO
Bardolino
Soave

Trieste •

PIEDMONT

Po

• Venice

Asti Spumante
Barolo

EMILIA-ROMAGNA

Genoa •

Bologna •

ADRIATIC SEA

Pisa •

Florence •

• Ancona

Arno

Verdicchio

TUSCANY

Perugia

Chianti

UMBRIA

A
P
E
N
N
I
N
E
S

LATIUM

• Rome

ITALY

PUGLIA

SARDINIA

CAMPANIA

Naples •

• Potenza

SANSOVINO
VINO BIANCO
WHITE TABLE WINE
PRODUCE OF ITALY
1.5 LITRES   e

SANSOVINO
VINO ROSSO
RED TABLE WINE
PRODUCE OF ITALY
1.5 LITRES

VINO ROSSO

Domari
Italian
Red Table Wine

PRODUCE OF ITALY   70 cl

Shipped and Bottled by
T'VANS MARSHALL & CO 163 REGENT STREET LONDON W1

• Palermo

SICILY
Corvo
Marsala

MEDITERRANEAN SEA

Main wine-producing areas

since that there were many I had missed. Yet there is a sort of family resemblance, however slight it may sometimes be, between the wines of Italy, just as there is a common quality of Italianateness between its peoples, hotly though Venetians and Neapolitans might sometimes deny it. And just as Italy is a country easy to love and the Italian people easy to like, the quality common to Italian wines is that they are easy to drink.

Italian wine is comparable to French wine in much the same way as the food of the two countries. Italian food is more akin to hearty French country cooking than to *haute cuisine*. (An Italian once said to me, 'We eat food, the French eat sauces.' It was unfair to the French but I knew what he meant.) Similarly, Italian wines are less subtle than the greatest wines of France and more akin to the non-aristocratic French wines.

Yet there are great wines among them. Barolo and the vintage Chiantis are full of character, fit companions for the great beefsteaks of Florence. Lighter reds such as Valpolicella and Bardolino are charmingly fresh with picnic lunches in the lake district that they come from, or with cold meats and salads at summertime suppers. Soave and Verdicchio are dry white wines that make delicate accompaniments to the fish-fries of Venice and I have sat long after dinner over the richly sweet, velvety Marsala of Sicily, whether served by the glass in its own right as a dessert wine or blended with egg-yolks into that best of all after-dinner sweets, *zabaglione*. One can linger even longer after dinner in Elban cafés over the island's Aleatico, as dark and as sweet as port, but not so cloying, and smelling deliciously of the Moscato grape. As does the light, sparkling Asti Spumante, sweet and fragrant, and delicious with a fig or a peach fresh from the tree.

All these, even the finest of them, are straightforward wines, easy to know. They are wines that wear their hearts on their sleeves, which is what is sometimes said of the Italians themselves, and which I consider a compliment, for it means that they are eager to be liked, both the wines and the people, and that is no bad thing.

It used to be alleged that Italian wines were carelessly made and inconsistent in quality. But since the Italian wine law came into force in 1965 a bottle labelled as DOC (*Denominazione di Origine Controllata*) contains as authentic a product as any French *appellation controlée* wine.

Another factor in the recent improvement in the quality and consistency of Italian wines has been the amount of government money that has gone into the development of Italy's poverty-stricken deep south – much of it into experimental vineyards, pest control and new presses and fermenting vats. Not so very long ago, the rough and ready wines of Sicily and Sardinia were used to 'stretch' the better-known wines of the north of Italy (and of the south of France). Now they stand on their own reputation, as Sicily's red and white Corvo wines bear witness on many a distinguished restaurant's wine-list.

It is wines such as these, as well as the more famous wines that I mentioned at the beginning of this section, that contribute to what has been described recently as an 'explosive growth' of Italian exports of wine. This is partly due to the effects of the now well-established Italian wine law, partly to an export drive by the Italian government and wine trade, but partly because wine-drinkers outside Italy have learned to know and to like them.

Spain and Portugal

One of the steps in the production of
sherry, in the Jerez area of Spain.
New wine is being extracted from the
barrel on the right to add to the old.

Spain

SPAIN HAS MORE LAND UNDER VINES THAN ANY OTHER COUNTRY IN Europe, although with rather less acreage of vineyards, France, Italy and the Soviet Union each produce more wine. However, of its more than four million acres of vineyard, it is a mere twenty thousand that have made Spain world-famous for one particular wine – sherry.

The name derives from the town of Jerez in the south-west. Like port, from the next-door country of Portugal, sherry is a fortified wine, which is to say that brandy is added to strengthen it. Sherry is about half as strong again, alcoholically, as claret or burgundy, and nearly twice the strength of a German wine. This is why sherry is served in small glasses and sipped, whether it is dry, as an aperitif, or sweet, as a dessert wine.

Palomino grapes – the grapes from which sherry is made – growing near Puerta de Santa Maria which, along with Jerez itself and San-Lucar, is one of the three great sherry towns.

Unlike that of the rest of Spain, the climate of the sherry country is consistent. This means that vintages, too, are constant, so that regular supplies of sherry are available every year exactly the same in style and quality as in previous years. This makes blending easy. The wines, in a series of casks of different years, are replenished one from another, the older from the younger. This is the *solera* system. It means that there is no such thing as a vintage sherry but that sherry, unlike unfortified table wines, can be controlled and standardised and sold under brand names that are guarantees not only of quality but of a continuing style.

Another sweet Spanish dessert wine is Malaga, strengthened and sweetened by the addition of concentrated grape juice to a dark, heavy richness. It is less well known in Britain than it used to be, but is still widely drunk by Germans, Belgians and Poles. They fortify themselves internally with bottled Spanish sunshine against the external grey, as the English, the Scandinavians and the Dutch do with sherry.

But if Malaga is less known than it used to be, the table wines of Spain are becoming better known and more are being exported as the prices of French wines rise.

The red wines of the Rioja region, in northern Spain, are dry, fruity and pleasing to the nose. There are lighter types, usually to be found in the same sort of bottles as claret, and heavier types, in burgundy-type bottles. The whites do not compare so well as the reds do with their French and German counterparts, being coarser.

Both reds and whites are grown in La Mancha, the Don Quixote country south of Madrid. Most of them are pretty ordinary wines, honest beverages, but without great distinction. But, Valdepeñas, the light red of the region, can be drunk young and cool, like Beaujolais, and can be similarly refreshing.

The best white wines of Spain, and what are probably its best sparklers, come from another corner of the country altogether – from Catalan Spain, in the extreme north-east, inland from Barcelona and the Costa Brava.

Holiday-makers here enjoy, with their fish dinners, the light, crisp white Marfil, and can make merry with the very dry sparkling wine of the Panades region, where the Condriou cellars are the biggest in Europe for sparkling wine – bigger than any in Champagne itself.

78

Down the coast is Tarragona, which gives its name to a strong, sweet red dessert wine – 'poor man's port' : Spain, in fact, produces every type of wine, and the outside world is becoming increasingly aware of the fact.

Spanish vineyards in the shadow of an ancient hilltop town. Spain has more land under vines than any other country.

Portugal

PORTUGAL, TOO, IS BEST KNOWN FOR ITS FORTIFIED WINE – IN HER CASE, port. When I first visited the port country, it was to celebrate the three-hundredth birthday of an Anglo-Scottish firm, for British roots in the port trade go very deep, and Oporto is strongly influenced – architecturally, socially and

TOP LEFT *Partially fermented red wine is run off into a barrel containing brandy, to make port.*
ABOVE *Port maturing in casks at Oporto, Portugal.*

VALDEORRAS

RIBEIRO

MINHO

VINHOS VERDES

DOURO

Oporto

Douro

DAO

Mondego

PORTUGAL

Te

Lisbon

SETUBAL

ATLANTIC
OCEAN

HUELVA

Seville

JER

Jerez de la Frontera

QUINTA
TAMARIZ
FINE OLD RUBY
PORT

BILBAO

PYRENEES

RIOJA

ALELLA

PANADES • Barcelona

Saragossa

CARIÑENA

PRIORATO
TARRAGONA
Ebro

SPAIN

Madrid •

MENTRIDA

UTIEL-REQUENA

Valencia

MANCHA

CHESTE

MANCHUELA

VALENCIA

VALDEPEÑAS

ALMANSA

JUMILLA

Alicante •

Cordoba •

MEDITERRANEAN SEA

alquivir

MONTILLA-MORILES

MALAGA

SIERRA NEVADA

Malaga

Main wine-producing areas

Castella
MEDIUM WHITE WINE
Produce of Spain
*Well balanced, fragrant and refreshing.
Serve chilled as a perfect accompaniment to white
meats and fish or on its own as an aperitif.*
70cl.   e
Victoria Wine
*Selected and bottled by Victoria Wine Co. Ltd.
London SW1*

CAMELIA
FINE OLD
**CREAM
SHERRY**
SHIPPED BY
MARTINEZ
EST.
PUERTO DE SANTA MARIA
PRODUCE OF SPAIN

PRODUCE ⊕ OF SPAIN
Finest Quality
TARRAGONA
SPANISH FULL SWEET
ESTABLISHED 1760
SHIPPED BY TAPLOWS LIMITED
LONDON W.1.

Tawny port from one of the Douro's best-known quintas – *the decanter is Victorian in style.*

economically – by the British connection. So, too, is Portugal's isle of Madeira.

But not all Portugal's wine is port. This tiny country, smaller than England, produces more than two hundred million gallons of wine a year – the seventh largest output in the world – of which only one bottle in fifty is port. And, averaged over the years, only one in a hundred bottles of port is vintage port. It may be that it is the great prestige of vintage that causes us to take port so seriously in this country.

More and more, though, Portugal has become important as a producer of light beverage wine to drink with meals, and not only of the rich, fortified ports and madeiras. Red, rosé, dry white and sweet white wines are now exported from the Estremadura region, just north of Lisbon. Between Lisbon and Oporto is the wild, mountainous, thickly wooded Dão region from clearings in which come strong, heavy red wines that are more like burgundy than claret and more like Rhône wines, such as Châteauneuf du Pape, than either. '*Tinto*' is the Portuguese for 'red', '*branco*' for 'white'. Dão Branco is not so easily come across as Dão Tinto. It is to be found in Britain, and is worth looking for, especially by those who like the burgundy rather than the hock type of white wine, for it is considerably cheaper than white burgundy, yet with something of the same character – full of flavour, yet very dry.

This, though, is to define Portuguese wines in terms of French, whereas the most interesting Portuguese table wines are the *vinhos verdes*. They are the most interesting because, like ports and madeiras, they are the most individually characteristic. No other country produces anything quite like them.

Vinhos verdes, green wines, are so called not because they are green in colour – they are white – but because they are 'green' in age. They are made from grapes that are picked young, and they are drunk young. For that matter, though this has nothing to do with their name, they are grown and made in the greenest part of Portugal. It lies between Oporto and the Minho river, which forms Portugal's northern frontier, and is a rainy, hilly, wooded region, very different from the wild, parched, rocky country that produces port. The early picking of the grapes results in a secondary fermentation after the wine is in bottle and this causes a very slight sparkle. It is not enough to attract the extra duty levied on fully sparkling wine, such as champagne, but enough to make *vinhos verdes* crisp and refreshing, especially if they are served very cool, and admirable for summer drinking. The Portuguese government has officially delimited the area in which these charming wines are grown, and the genuine article bears a paper seal over its cork.

Finally, two less well-known but to me very interesting wines. Grandjo is a sweet white wine that Edward VII was very fond of, which I can commend to those who like a Sauternes or a Barsac with fruit after dinner. It has something of the same fragrance and delicacy and is quite a lot cheaper. At the other end of the sweetness scale are the wines of Vila Real, which are so dry that in some wine-lists they are noted as being suitable (subject to doctor's approval, of course) for diabetics.

It is a remarkable country that produces wines so luscious as port, so austere as the dry Vila Reals, and so gay and individual as the *vinhos verdes*.

82

Mediterranean Shores
The Levant and North Africa

*A cheerful family group at grape-
picking time in a Cretan vineyard.*

ABOVE *Resin drips from incisions in the bark of pine-trees and is added to some Greek wines which, when thus treated, are known as retsina.*

THE MEDITERRANEAN SEA IS ALMOST ENTIRELY SURROUNDED BY VINE-yards. From Spain, by way of the south of France, to Italy and its islands; up the Adriatic to Yugoslavia; round the deeply indented coasts of Greece to Bulgaria and Turkey; the Levant and the long North African shore – everywhere there is wine, except possibly among the fiercely Muslim mountaineers of Albania. There is even wine in Egypt, which has won prizes, been exported to the Soviet Union, and some of which has been set before the present writer in a bottle labelled 'Clos des Pyramides'. The wine of Spain, France and Italy we have already discussed, and those of Yugoslavia and Bulgaria have been touched upon. Mention, at least, must be made of others.

Greece is known chiefly for its retsina. This white or pink wine has pine-tree resin, milk-white and tacky to the finger, added to it, giving a taste of turpentine, which you like or dislike intensely. The Greeks themselves seem to love it less than they used to. The proportion of resinated to unresinated wine produced in recent years has fallen dramatically, and what wines they do resinate are less heavily treated than of old. This may be because the demand by tourists for wines more like ones they are used to has prompted the Greeks to make wines that need no resin, and they have taken to them themselves.

Not that the taste for, or the production of, retsina has ever been spread over the whole of Greece. What retsina there is comes from the middle of Attica itself, and it is Athenians who like it. Macedonia, in northern Greece, produces good, heart-warming reds such as Naoussa, and so does the island of Crete. Another island, Samos, produces a sound dry white and a sweet muscat. For consistency, the visitor should look in the tavernas' wine-lists for the white Pallini Alpha and the red and white Demestica. Mavrodaphne is a richly sweet dessert wine.

Greece's traditional enemy, Turkey, is one of the world's greatest grape-growing nations, but most of the grapes are for eating, not for drinking. All the same, there is some Turkish wine, and it is not to be sneezed at. The red and white Trakia wines are named, like the similarly styled Bulgarian wines, after the ancient Roman province of Thrace. They are grown in the European section of Turkey. The fuller red Buzbag comes from Anatolia itself, south-east of Ankara.

The most important wine-growing country of the eastern and southern Mediterranean is the island of Cyprus which, in spite of its troubles, is one of the most go-ahead of all such countries. Vast wineries have been established, and extensive vineyards planted in the south-west, near Limassol and Paphos, and there are even pipe-lines from wine-making plants on the coast that run for half a mile or so under the sea and deliver ten thousand gallons an hour into ships lying offshore. I was there once to see a million and a half litres of dry and sweet 'sherry' and a rich dessert wine, Commandaria, pumped into a French tanker. And the French know good wine when they see it.

There are decent, sturdy reds in the island, and white and rosé wines much drier and less coarse than one expects such wines that are grown in sunny southern latitudes to be. They are all flavour enough, though, to go with

OPPOSITE *Vines spectacularly set among the conical dwellings of Turkish Cappadocia. But the Turks, mainly Muslim, drink little wine themselves.*

84

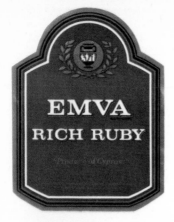

EMVA RICH RUBY

EMVA RICH GOLDEN CYPRUS SHERRY

Roditis ROSÉ TABLE WINE

RETSINA

ACHAIA CLAUSS DEMESTICA

BELOW *Terraced vineyards and almond trees in blossom in the Troodos mountains, Cyprus.*
RIGHT *A shop-full of Cretan-made wines in Heraklion, capital of Crete.*

Main wine-producing areas

Tunis

Algiers

Oran

ALGERIA

TUNISIA

Casablanca

Fez

ATLAS MOUNTAINS

MOROCCO

Marrakesh

•Rostov

UKRAINE

•Krasnodor

CAUCASUS MOUNTAINS

GEORGIA

Odessa•

CRIMEA

•Sebastopol

BLACK SEA

EAST AND NORTH-EAST ANATOLIA

ROMANIA

TRANSYLVANIAN
ALPS

Bucharest•

CENTRAL ANATOLIA

BULGARIA

BALKAN
MOUNTAINS

Istanbul•

TURKEY

GOSLAVIA

•Sofia

THRACE

SOUTH AND EAST ANATOLIA

SYRIA

Thessaloniki•

AEGEAN

Izmir•

THESSALY

SEA

AEGEAN COAST

CYPRUS

•Nicosia

GREECE

Beirut•

•Damascus

Athens•

LEBANON

PELOPONNESE

Tel Aviv•

•Amman

Jerusalem•

JORDAN

CRETE

•Heraklion

ISRAEL

MEDITERRANEAN SEA

RED SEA

LIBYA

EGYPT

Chemison wine cellars near Bethlehem, in Israel. Wine was grown in Israel in biblical times, but the vineyards of today date from the 1880s: these cellars near Bethlehem have an old-world look about them.

the rich and spicy Greek-Cypriot cooking. Particularly, besides the heavy dessert 'sherries' marketed in Britain under best-selling brand names, Cyprus produces a pale dry 'sherry'. It is made and matured in exactly the same way that a Spanish sherry is made and matured, and I have heard of two English Masters of Wine (holders, that is, of the highest qualification a wine-merchant can earn, and the equivalent to a university degree) who, tasting blind, mistook a Cyprus fino for a Spanish, commenting afterwards on its 'uncanny resemblance'.

A modest amount of wine is grown in Syria – vineyards are interspersed with tobacco plantations in Latakia. A great deal more is produced in the Lebanon, where a dry white wine, grown in the hills above Beirut, goes well with the huge local *langoustes*. When British troops were in Jordan, in 1958, the name of the local red wine, Latroun, gave rise to some soldierly jests: it is better than it sounds. In Muslim countries such as this there are plenty of wine-drinkers to maintain that the Prophet was not against wine, but merely against its abuse. In any case, non-Muslim tourists demand wine, and who would deny a tourist?

In Israel, curiously enough, where Judaism does not at all forbid wine – indeed, wine is a part of its festivals, especially the Passover – very little is drunk, except on such religious occasions. However, some very respectable wine is grown. A high proportion of visiting tourists are American Jews, not themselves big wine-drinkers, but a good deal is shipped to the United States, all the same. In 1882, when enthusiastic Zionists, most of them from Russia, were first settling in Palestine, a French Rothschild set up vineyards and wineries at Rishon-le-Zion, where skilled Israeli wine-makers trained in France and Germany are now in charge. There should be a great future for Israeli wines. Meanwhile, sound table wines are being made from French varieties of grape. The red Adom Atic and the white Carmel 'hock', so-called, are worth anyone's attention, and 'The President's' sparkling wine must be one of the best of its kind east of Italy.

It is Jews, oddly enough, and Russian refugees, who grow the wine in Iran, where they seem sterner about alcohol than their fellow-Muslims of the Arab countries. But quite an amount of wine gets put away by the Iranians, to say nothing of arack and the local vodka. After all, some of the world's best caviar comes from Iranian waters, and what else can you drink with caviar?

There is tolerable red wine to be found in Libya, grown in vineyards originally planted by Mussolini's Italian settlers. Very sound wines indeed are grown in Tunisia, where the former Italian and French vineyards have now been expropriated but are still run with advice from Italian experts. Excellent Moroccan reds have figured in lists no less august than those of Fortnum and Mason, but the biggest and most advanced North African wine-growing country is undoubtedly Algeria. This was once part of metropolitan France, the wines of which were shipped, quite legitimately, as 'Produce of France' and were entitled by French law, because of their quality, to style themselves VDQS – *vins délimités de qualité superieure*. Big, mouth-filling reds are the Algerian speciality, many of them imported by the French to give backbone to the thin, sharp reds of the Midi. But many are worthy of respect in their own right.

Eastern Europe

Tokay, one of Hungary's best-known wines. The Tokay hills are ancient volcanoes, and the soil here — lava covered with sandy loam — is perfect for vines.

MUCH OF EASTERN EUROPE WAS ONCE IN THE ROMAN EMPIRE AND
has grown wine for centuries. Thrace, for instance, which is now in
Bulgaria, gives its ancient name, Trakia, to very drinkable red and white
wines; and ancient Illyria, which is now north-western Yugoslavia, produces
the white Riesling which is the post-war success story of wine-drinking
Europe. Romania is so called because its people were Latins islanded in a sea
of Slavs. There, too, wine-growing is an ancient way of life, and some

*Part of a vineyard in Yugoslavia
near Metlika, Croatia.*

delightful wines – the whites especially – are grown in most parts of the country. Those of Tirnave, north of the Carpathian mountains, and of Murfatlar, almost on the Black sea coast, are outstanding. The Carpathians sweep in a great curve northwards into Czechoslavakia, which has pleasant wines of its own, as well as the best beer in the world – Pilsener – and I have drunk a decent enough Moravian Riesling by the glass in a Prague wine-cellar.

Main wine-producing areas

The great wine-growing surprise of Eastern Europe, though, is the Soviet Union itself, where production has increased something like fourfold since the war, to make it the third or fourth greatest wine-producing country in the world. It is twenty years and more since the government decided that it was more *kulturny* (cultured), and more healthy, to be a wine-drinking rather than a vodka-drinking country. They began to look for types of vines that would flourish outside such traditional southern regions as Armenia, Georgia and the Crimea, where wine has been made since Roman times. So hybrid strains have been developed that are yielding sound wines in Soviet Central Asia, in Moldavia and the Ukraine. Classic French and German strains have also been imported, to yield fairly run-of-the-mill Cabernets and Rieslings.

Soviet agronomic enterprise may well do much in the not-too-distant future to provide Europe's wine-drinkers with plenty of sound wine of moderate quality at modest prices. Meanwhile, the interesting Soviet wines for the enquiring wine-lover are not those that are Russian versions of wines that can be found elsewhere, and better, but the wines grown nowhere else, and now exported. Among these are the white Tsinandali of Georgia, which is dry, clean and appetising; the dry red, very full-flavoured Mukuzani, also of Georgia; and the fragrant, crisp, deep pink, or lightish red, Negri de Purkar of the Moldavian Soviet Republic.

· But if it is the Slavonic countries of Eastern Europe – Yugoslavia and the Soviet Union – that are setting the pace in these parts in increasing production, it is Hungary, not Slavonic but Magyar, that is still the most interesting.

Hungary has always been a great wine-growing country, and Balatoni Riesling from the shores of that vast inland sea, Lake Balaton, has long been known abroad. From between the lake and Budapest comes a drier white wine from a native grape, the Mori Dry. It is as characteristically Hungarian as the romantically named Bull's Blood of Eger, a red wine so deep in colour as to be almost black, and with remarkable depth of flavour.

Most famous of all, though, is Tokay, from the village of that name in the far north-east of Hungary, almost on the Soviet frontier. There is a dry, rather heavy, white Tokay, called Szamarodni. If the grapes are attacked by the 'noble rot' that turns them almost into sultanas – the same process that produces the great sweet Sauternes of France – then the wine is not Szamarodni but Aszu, its sweetness measured by the number of 'puttonyos' (hods) of the sweet rich pulp added to each cask. A five-puttonyos Tokay Aszu is a golden, luscious, intensely fragrant dessert wine, and a great experience.

Greater still is the Tokay Essenz (Tokay essence) itself, made from the rich juice that drips from individually picked overripe grapes under the pressure of their own weight. A clear, golden, liqueur-like wine, immensely sweet, extremely expensive, it is credited with all sorts of therapeutic, not to say aphrodisiac, qualities. It was said of an old friend of mine who, mindful of its reputation as a restorative, long treasured a small bottle, instructing his family that when he lay dying the essence should be applied to his lips. When eventually he was at death's door, the wine was duly applied. He did not recover. I wish he had done. But, the family told me, he died smiling.

A medium dry white wine made with Laški Riesling grapes from vineyards in the Podravski region of Slovenia Best served chilled

Yugoslav· Laški Riesling

Alcohol 11% by volume Contents 70cl ℮

Specially bottled for Marks & Spencer Ltd Baker Street London

92

North America

*In New York State, unlike
California, wine is made from the
native American grape, here seen being
vintaged.*

ONCE UPON A TIME, I WAS A FOREIGN CORRESPONDENT AND HAD TO concern myself, on behalf of my newspaper, with the comings and goings of world statesmen. When I reported on the official meeting in Vienna of President Kennedy and Mr Khrushchev, I gave myself and my readers some light relief from high diplomacy by furnishing details of the luncheons to which they entertained each other in their countries' respective embassies. The Russians offered vodka and Soviet wines with their own national dishes, but the Americans served French wine only – Château Mouton-Rothschild 1953, indeed – with the main course. Mr Khrushchev scored, no doubt, with his caviar, but had President Kennedy matched Californian wines against Crimean he would have been an easy winner.

The sad thing, as I observed at the time, is that some Americans do not seem to have the confidence in Californian wines that the wines and their makers deserve. They are underestimated even in their own country, where too much prestige in the matter of wine attaches itself to 'imported' as against 'domestic': I have noticed, more than once, in New York that an inferior 'imported' French or Italian wine has been preferred to a classic 'domestic', from California.

Harvesting grapes in the Napa valley, California. The town of Napa is about 30 miles north-east of San Francisco, and this area produces some of California's most distinguished wines.

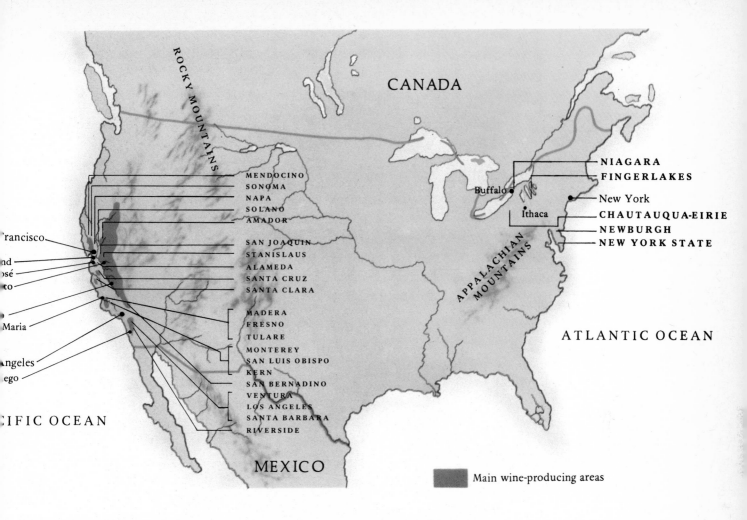

ROCKY MOUNTAINS

CANADA

APPALACHIAN MOUNTAINS

ATLANTIC OCEAN

MEXICO

Buffalo
Ithaca

NIAGARA
FINGERLAKES
New York
CHAUTAUQUA-EIRIE
NEWBURGH
NEW YORK STATE

MENDOCINO
SONOMA
NAPA
SOLANO
AMADOR
SAN JOAQUIN
STANISLAUS
ALAMEDA
SANTA CRUZ
SANTA CLARA
MADERA
FRESNO
TULARE
MONTEREY
SAN LUIS OBISPO
KERN
SAN BERNADINO
VENTURA
LOS ANGELES
SANTA BARBARA
RIVERSIDE

rancisco
nd
osé
to
Maria
Angeles
ego

IFIC OCEAN

Main wine-producing areas

Note that I refer not to United States wines in general but to Californian wines in particular. Wine is made in more than half a dozen other states in the union, notably in New York State and in Ohio, but from the native North-American grape, *vitis labrusca*, and not from the wine-vine, *vitis vinifera*, cultivated in Europe. These wines from American vines have a distinctive flavour of their own that is distasteful to palates conditioned by the wines of France and Germany. It is a curious earthy but sweet back-taste that the French call 'foxy'.

It is surprising, therefore, that it is on the root stocks of native American vines that the so-called 'noble' vines of Europe, producing the great clarets and hocks and burgundies, are now grafted. This is as a precaution against the phylloxera pest, to which native American vines are resistant and European vines are not.

In California, as in Europe, wines are made from the classic European vines grafted on to American roots. More and more the Californian growers are naming their wines after the grapes they come from. These are called 'varietal' wines. They are produced from grapes such as the Riesling, which produces the finest German and Alsatian wines; the Pinot Noir, to which we owe red burgundy; and the Chardonnay, which produces the white burgundies. In different soils and under different suns, of course, the same grapes will produce wines of different character. A Yugoslav Riesling, for instance, is comparable with, but really different from, a German Riesling.

95

Similarly a Californian Cabernet will not smell or taste or age in the bottle in quite the same way as claret, though it be made with the same care and expert knowledge. In my experience, Californian wines tend in general to be rather fuller and rounder than French wines from the same grapes, probably because of the greater intensity of Californian sunshine. Yet they are without the coarseness of some wines from hotter wine-growing regions such as Spain and North Africa.

Californian wines cannot be cheap outside their own region, because of transport costs and rates of exchange, and because the labour costs are by no means the lowest in the world. So opportunities to taste a wide range of Californian wines are limited. Some British shippers do list, among other Californians, a Sylvaner, a Riesling, a Chardonnay and a Chenin Blanc. These are all white and all with considerable intensity of flavour, resembling their German, Alsatian and Burgundian counterparts but with an extra punch to the flavour, and yet with a clean, crisp finish. Of the reds, the Californian Cabernet Sauvignon is subtler and more elegant than the Californian Gamay, but then the same is true of a claret and a Beaujolais, from those same respective grapes.

At their best, Californian wines can be compared with the best that Europe can produce, and it is good to learn that the Californian acreage under vines is rapidly increasing. Parts, for instance, of Monterey County, which enjoy every wine-growing advantage except an adequate rainfall, are now being irrigated by overhead sprinklers fed from mountain reservoirs to give controlled rainfall, as required. Mother Nature is being given a helping hand by Uncle Sam, and we wine-lovers can be grateful for this family teamwork.

Vine leaves take on the red and russet of autumn in a Californian vineyard.

Canada is not known at all in Europe as a wine-growing country, although she produces more than Yugoslavia or Greece and twice as much as Australia. This is because Canadian wine has the 'foxy' flavour of North-American vines. Most of it comes from the Niagara region between Lake Ontario and Lake Erie, but a little is grown, too, in British Columbia. Chiefly, it is sweet fortified wine from the native North-American grape, and it is not to the European taste. But production is expanding, and classic European strains are being introduced, so Canada will eventually loom large in the wine-lists.

When it does, the leaders in the field will undoubtedly be the dry white table wines and the dry sparkling wine now made in the Niagara Falls peninsula (part of the same wine-growing region as New York State's) from French Pinot Noir and Chardonnay stock. Another notable Canadian wine is the full and fragrant, but dry, white Gewürztraminer from the same grape as the famous Alsatian wine.

It is interesting that a dozen years and more ago, Britain's greatest expert on experimental vineyards and hybrid grapes prophesied that Canada and the Soviet Union would both become leading wine-growing countries, because of the time, money and spirit of enterprise they were devoting to expansion and experiment. Both countries have increased production enormously since then, and in the table of the world's forty-five wine-producing countries, the Soviet Union lies third, and Canada eleventh.

South America

Workers in Chilean vineyards. Chile
grows wine for nearly two thousand of
its three thousand miles of length.

AS BEFITS THE GREATEST BEEF-EATING COUNTRY IN THE WORLD, Argentina is pretty nearly the greatest wine-drinking country, perhaps the greatest. An Argentinian's annual consumption of ninety litres falls short of the one hundred and ten litres per person consumed on average by the Frenchman and the Italian. However, it must be remembered that consumption by tourists must necessarily be included in a national total, and that France and Italy entertain far more tourists per head of population than Argentina. This is a major reason why, although Argentina lies third or fourth in the table of world producers, she has never loomed large as an exporter. What the Argentinian grows, he guzzles.

This is changing. When I was in Argentina for a recent vintage, I watched them gather grapes which, to European eyes, seemed enormous in size. In their sun-drenched vineyards, from which one could see the snow-capped peaks of the Andes, I learned that improved methods, together with the expansion of wine-growing areas, now combine to provide an exportable surplus. Capital investment in huge, modern wineries keeps pace with this.

Chile is so narrow a country, between the Andes and the Pacific, that virtually all its vineyards have a mountainous background.

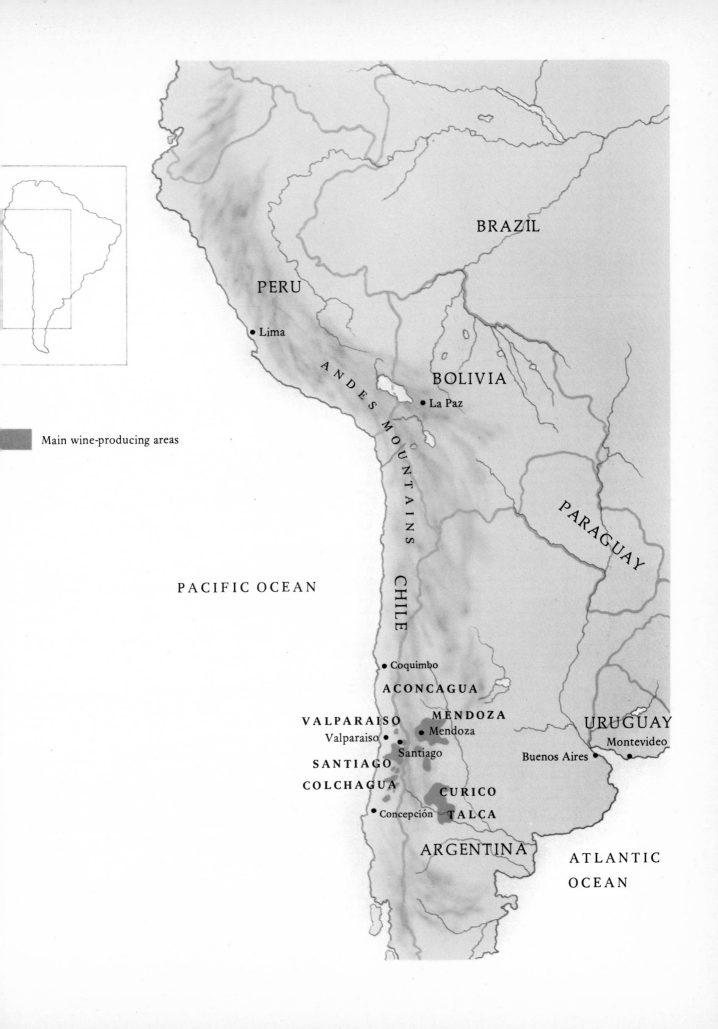

Main wine-producing areas

BRAZIL

PERU

• Lima

BOLIVIA

• La Paz

PARAGUAY

PACIFIC OCEAN

ANDES MOUNTAINS

CHILE

• Coquimbo

ACONCAGUA

VALPARAISO

MENDOZA

Valparaiso •

• Mendoza

URUGUAY

SANTIAGO

• Santiago

Montevideo •

COLCHAGUA

Buenos Aires •

CURICO

• Concepción

TALCA

ARGENTINA

ATLANTIC OCEAN

The biggest wine-tank in the world was recently built at Mendoza, the capital of Argentinian wine-growing, costing £5 million, insured against earthquakes, and holding five and a quarter million litres.

What is now regarded there as a native grape, the Criolla, is probably a descendant of various types brought by sixteenth-century Jesuit missionaries. These vines were crossed with each other and are now producing big grapes in enormous bunches. I heard of a bunch weighing twelve and a half pounds. They are used both as table grapes and to produce the local, cheap *vin ordinaire*.

But we owe the finer wines of the country to nineteenth-century Italian immigrants and the classic vines of Europe. The Italians of the 1880s and thereabouts used the melting snows of the Andes to irrigate the desert region around Mendoza. Here they and their descendants planted the same varieties of vine that produce such classic French and German wines as hock, Moselle, the great Alsatian wines, burgundy and claret. The Malbec grape, a minor contribution to the great clarets, is especially successful in Argentina. Happily, in a beef-eating country, the reds are better and more numerous than the whites.

The wine-growing region of Argentina is roughly as far from the equator as those of North Africa, so this is a hotter area than the wine-growing regions of France and Germany. But hot-country wines need not be coarse. The effects of latitude can be offset by altitude. Some of the finest wines of Italy are grown a couple of thousand feet above sea-level, and so are those of Argentina. Another way of ensuring that too much sunshine does not coarsen the grape is by training the vines so that the bunches are shaded by the leaves from the sun's direct, midday rays. So even the whites, though not perhaps so consistently successful as the reds, are sometimes lighter and more delicate than one would expect from so near the equator. I have enjoyed, especially, one made from a blend of the French, white Pinot grape and the German Riesling, and a very good rosé blended from the Alsatian Pinot Gris grape and the Bordeaux Sémillon. But the reds made from the Malbec and the Cabernet grapes, which go into claret, are probably Argentina's best.

High-altitude wine-growing in low latitudes is also done in Chile. Across the Andes, Chile grows wine for more than half of the three-thousand-mile coastal strip it consists of. The best, however, come from foothill and river-valley country near Santiago, in the middle, and from European varieties of grape – notably the French Cabernet and the German Riesling. Indeed, some of the best reds I have ever come across from outside Europe have been Chilean Cabernets imported by knowledgeable London shippers. They are well worth looking out for, and giving more bottle-age once one has bought them. These wines are cheap because, I am sorry to say, of low labour costs; the profit margin does not make it worth while for shippers and merchants to put them away for the maturing they need, but makes it very definitely worth while for the consumer to forgo a few months' interest on his money.

Of the rest of South, and Central, America's wines, all that need to be said is that Mexico produces some, and Brazil and Uruguay quite a lot. Mexico also imports California wines, and the others wine from Argentina and Chile. Very sensible of them.

Some of the New World's finest wines come from French classic varieties of grapes grown in Chile, where this vintage scene was pictured.

Australia, New Zealand and South Africa

*Vineyards at Stellenbosch, inland from
Cape Town and Table Mountain,
where wine has been grown since the
days of der Stel, second Dutch governor
of Cape Province.*

THE GRAPE-VINE'S NEAR-EASTERN BEGINNINGS GO BACK BEYOND recorded history. Noah cannot have been the first Levantine of whom it could be said that 'he drank of the wine, and was drunken'. But we know almost to the day when wine began to be grown in Australia, for Captain Arthur Phillip landed at Sydney on 26 January 1788, with 'plants for the settlement'. He planted vines, presumably within the next few days, at Farm Cove, where the Botanical Gardens are now.

Many of today's great Australian vineyards have long ago celebrated their centenaries, and some are not all that far off their double hundred – not so long, perhaps, in the history of wine itself, but older than many of the vineyards of the old world. There are plenty of younger ones in France itself. There is much inherited skill and experience in Australian wine-making, as well as a benign climate and suitable soil, especially in the valleys of the Hunter and the Murray rivers, and the Barossa valley. These valleys are all in the south-east of the continent, in New South Wales, Victoria and South Australia.

Vintage time in the Swan Valley, Australia. The Western Australian vineyards, including those of Swan Valley, are some of the newest in Australia, although wine production began in the country in the 1820s.

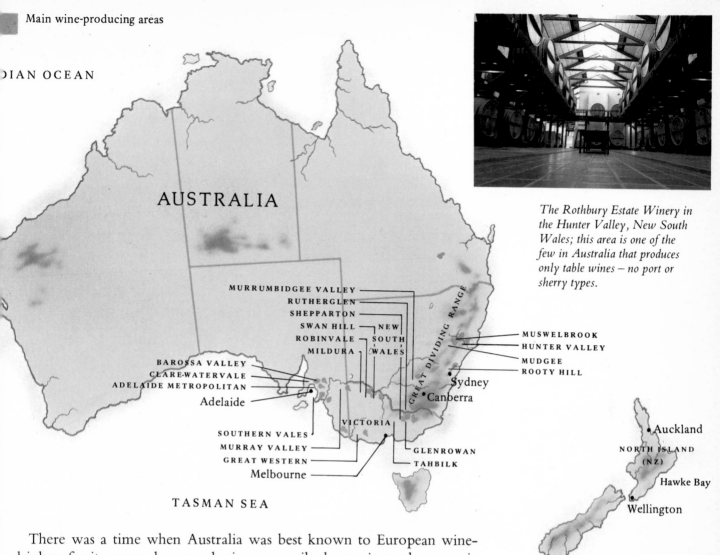

AUSTRALIA

DIAN OCEAN

MURRUMBIDGEE VALLEY
RUTHERGLEN
SHEPPARTON
SWAN HILL — NEW
ROBINVALE — SOUTH
MILDURA — WALES

BAROSSA VALLEY
CLARE-WATERVALE
ADELAIDE METROPOLITAN
Adelaide

MUSWELBROOK
HUNTER VALLEY
MUDGEE
ROOTY HILL

GREAT DIVIDING RANGE

Sydney
Canberra

VICTORIA

SOUTHERN VALES
MURRAY VALLEY
GREAT WESTERN
Melbourne

GLENROWAN
TAHBILK

TASMAN SEA

Auckland

NORTH ISLAND
(NZ)

Hawke Bay

Wellington

The Rothbury Estate Winery in the Hunter Valley, New South Wales; this area is one of the few in Australia that produces only table wines – no port or sherry types.

There was a time when Australia was best known to European wine-drinkers for its coarse, heavy red wines, prescribed as tonics to the anaemic because of their iron content. They did not commend themselves to connoisseurs. Now, although there are still plenty of these Australian so-called 'burgundies' to be found, the best Australian vineyards are producing better balanced reds. Many of them are produced from such classic French grapes as the Cabernet, from which are made the finest clarets, and the Shiraz, which in the Rhône valley (as the Syrah) produces the great red Hermitage.

Australian nomenclature is confusing: some wines are sold under a firm's name, some under fancy brand names, some under place-names and some as 'varietal' wines, after their grape. As the climate is so consistent, vintage dates are unimportant save as indications of age.

Most European wine-lovers, looking objectively at Australian wines, speak with especial respect of the reds of Rutherglen, in the Murray River valley, which divides New South Wales and Victoria; also those of Stonyfell, from South Australia, have a good reputation. The Tahbilk Cabernet and the Mildara Cabernet-Shiraz are outstanding. If they have any faults, these high-quality Australian reds, they are a lack of bouquet to match their depth of flavour and colour, and also a tendency to age rather quickly in the bottle. Once they have reached their peak, these wines 'thin out' sooner than would be expected by those used to cellaring French wines. But so long as one knows what to expect, one buys and consumes accordingly.

Australian whites have come up in the world, and some light and elegant wines are being made from the Rhine Riesling, especially at Coonawarra in South Australia and in the Barossa valley. Also I have tasted in London, and enjoyed, a wine called Leonay Rinegold, a charming medium-sweetish light wine, very like a German wine, and a Tahbilk 'hock', so called even though it is made from the French Hermitage grape. European vines change their character in Australian soil and under Australian skies, and it is more like a hock from the Rhine than a wine from the Rhône.

There are Australian fortified wines of the sherry type and of the port type, and there are sparkling wines of which Seppelt's Great Western is probably the best and certainly the best known. It comes from hilly country north-west of Melbourne, and should not be confused with the American sparkling wine of the same name, from New York State, to which it is greatly superior.

A European wine-lover could emigrate to Australia and remain a very happy man so long as he remembered not to cellar his red wines for as long as he would at home and that taste matters more than smell. An English friend, long settled in Australia, once wrote to me: 'When I think of Australian wine I do not think of an elegant dinner-table with men and women slowly savouring each glass. I think of picnics in the bush with the red wine warming in the sunshine or the white wine cooling in the creek and glasses laid out on the rocks where the lizards flick and rustle. At those times and in those conditions it is as good as any wine in the world.'

Modern methods of production at Corbans vineyard, New Zealand.

Wine-growing in New Zealand has nearly as long a history. Samuel Marsden, a missionary to the Maoris, planted vines as long ago as 1819 in North Island, where soil and climate are as favourable as in the best regions of France. French and German vines do well, but for many a long year wine-production did not flourish. New Zealanders, on the whole, did not want the light table wines that their country was best fitted to produce – they wanted tea or port.

Since the war, however, production has increased enormously, from eighty-five thousand gallons a year to nearly five million gallons. The late André Simon, famous founder of the Wine and Food Society, reported more than favourably in the 1960s on a New Zealand white wine made from the German Müller-Thurgau grape and described a red wine made from the French Cabernet as 'a fine wine by any standard'. Importing countries may congratulate themselves, because New Zealand has recently become a wine-exporting country.

Fine New Zealand wines – two red, a white and a semi-sparkling rosé – appeared for the first time on a British wine-shipper's list in the winter of 1977–8. To wine-drinkers whose tastes have been formed by European wines in general, and by French wines in particular (and this includes wine-drinkers in the United States, Australia and elsewhere) there is no doubt that the outstanding New Zealand wine is the red Cabernet Sauvignon, made from the same grape as the great clarets and some of the finest Californian wines.

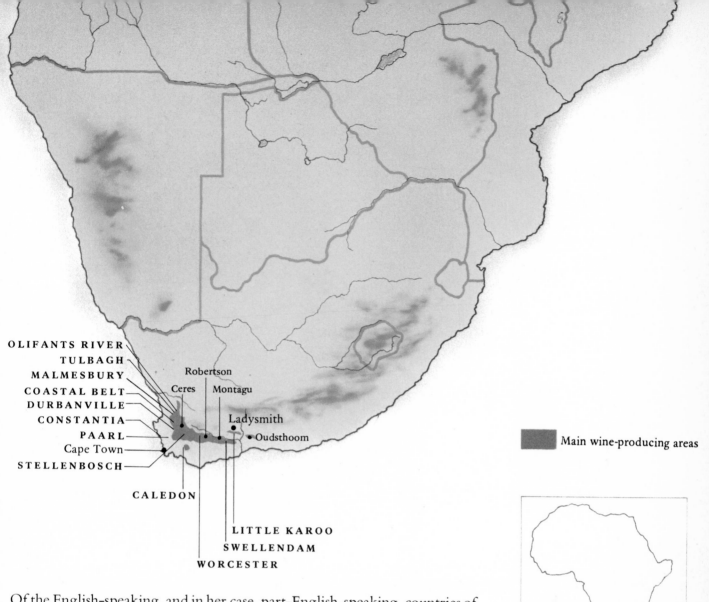

OLIFANTS RIVER
TULBAGH
MALMESBURY
COASTAL BELT
DURBANVILLE
CONSTANTIA
PAARL
Cape Town
STELLENBOSCH

Robertson
Ceres   Montagu

Ladysmith
Oudsthoom

CALEDON

LITTLE KAROO
SWELLENDAM
WORCESTER

Main wine-producing areas

Of the English-speaking, and in her case, part-English-speaking, countries of the Southern Hemisphere, South Africa has the longest wine-growing history. Vines were planted by the first Dutch settlers in 1655, and the French Huguenots, who arrived after the Revocation of the Edict of Nantes a mere generation later, developed the vineyards and the wine trade. Cape wines – especially the dessert wine, Constantia – were famous in Britain from the Napoleonic wars. Then Gladstone's budget of 1860 reduced the duty on French wines to the level of that on Cape wines, which had been only half the price. Imperial preference was reintroduced in 1925, but now no longer applies, because of EEC requirements.

Meanwhile, the strength of the industry lies in its fortified wines and in those that go to the distilleries. The climate of the Cape is especially suitable for wines to be made after the style of sherry and of port. The sherry types are the most successful or, at any rate, nearer to the European prototype.

There would be a greater production, no doubt, of the Cape's sound red and white table wines, well made from European grape varieties, were South Africa more of a wine-drinking nation. White South Africans are brandy-drinkers, the heaviest in the world I am told, and graciously permit the African himself to drink 'native beer'. Perhaps, in time, South Africa will become the world's first black wine-growing, wine-drinking, nation.

Choosing and Keeping Your Wines

*The light shining through this glass
reveals a clear, glowing white wine.*

OPPOSITE *A wine tasting in a
German cellar.*

How to Choose Wine
and Where to Buy It

IT USED ALWAYS TO BE SAID, AND IT IS STILL LARGELY TRUE, THAT one should buy the most expensive wine that one can afford to get the best value. The reason behind this is that duty, taxes, bottling charges (including the bottle itself, cork, capsule and label), freight, insurance and general overheads are the same for every bottle of table wine; the same for every bottle of fortified wine; and the same for all sparklers. Sparkling wine pays a little more duty than still; fortified wine pays more than either because of greater alcoholic strength. Thus, in Britain, to take a specific example (other countries would present a similar picture), a bottle of wine costing £1 contains 20 pence worth of wine, but a bottle of wine costing £2 contains £1·20 worth. By paying twice as much per bottle, you get six times as much value in wine.

But, as I said above, this is only *largely* true. It is not entirely so. Some wine-merchants are greedier than others, or not such shrewd buyers, or are not, themselves, big and important enough to drive hard bargains with their suppliers. To look at vintage ports, for instance, and to take one particular vintage of one particular shipper. At the time of writing, one distinguished wine-merchant is asking half as much again for the Dow 1960 as a similarly distinguished firm. The advice always to buy the most expensive for the sake of good value hardly applies here.

Then there is the tyranny of vintage charts. Every child knows why a long hot English summer means splendid strawberries – but not so many of them. Also, not enough sun in the ripening period, and rain during the harvest,

Different ways to buy wine:
BELOW *Big names on display in the window of an established wine merchant.*
BELOW RIGHT *More and more supermarkets are now taking to selling wine as well.*

result in fruits that may look nice, but lack flavour and go mushy or mouldy soon after picking. It is for the same reasons that some years are bad for wine and others, when there has been enough sunshine, and the rain has come at the right time, are good. Some firms and societies publish little charts showing, by a system of stars or marks out of seven, which are the good, bad and indifferent years for claret, burgundy, champagne, hock and port. Take no notice of them.

First of all, unless we are millionaires, most of the wines we buy are non-vintage – probably sold under brand names – blended from the vintages of various years to strike a balance, maintain a consistent style, and be ready to drink when ready to sell. The vintage year is not mentioned on the label because it is not relevant. At the same time, some vineyards, because they picked just before a hailstorm that struck their neighbours, or because they face the sun better, or for one or many other reasons, make good wine in an 'off' year. Consequently, you can pay too much for the wine of a good year from a badly managed vineyard. The best shippers are shrewd enough to buy by taste, not by year. Also, wine of different years develops at different rates. A vintage chart may well show that the 1962 and the 1957 clarets were equally good, but it cannot show that the 1962 wines were ready to drink before the 1957 wines. A great wine of a great year will be harsh in the mouth if drunk too soon, thin and flabby if past its best.

Some years are very uneven. In 1964, the claret vineyards that picked before the autumn downpour made excellent wine. Others – and among them some of the very greatest, accustomed to waiting to the very last minute for the sake of extra ripeness – were badly caught, and their wines are disappointing. Finally, too much dependence on vintage charts has made the wines of good years too dear, because too much in demand. It must not be supposed that because they make the wines of other years cheaper this is

Modern methods: a grape-picking machine at a French wine co-operative at Salins du Midi. The vines are planted further apart than in the old days so that machines can pass between them.

Chevaliers du Tastevin, in their robes as members of Burgundy's renowned wine fraternity, hold a banquet in their headquarters at Clos de Vougeot. This trade fraternity was founded in 1933 and meets regularly for banquets.

necessarily to the consumer's advantage. If it puts a dedicated wine-grower into financial difficulties, or forces him to over-price his better wine, nobody benefits.

If you are in the market for the kind of wine in which vintage years matter, then you are spending a fair amount of money, and planning ahead. Better to seek out a good wine-merchant and ask his advice than fumble your way around the misleading landmarks of a vintage chart. Better still, seek out a couple, collate what they tell you and compare their prices.

If you are buying from big stores, supermarkets or the branches of chain wine-merchants, the vintage problem does not occur. At the same time there is no one behind a counter to advise if you pick your wine from a shelf. But such companies are wealthy enough to employ top tasters and shrewd buyers, and with their great spending power, they can buy advantageously and obtain the best value for money. They can buy their day-to-day table wines from similarly big co-operatives with modern and economical plants, and they can buy in bulk. Finer wines may be obtained from smaller growers by smaller wine-merchants, and in smaller quantities which the large concerns cannot be bothered with. However, this is not always true, and it is never the cheapest method of wholesale buying. Chain stores, and the like, do not sell wines for long-term laying-down (although they may come to it, and I hope they do) but they are better placed than many grander-sounding individual establishments to sell sound wine for present drinking.

Choice is really a matter of tasting as many wines as you possibly can, and not in the way a professional taster goes about his job. He tastes a score or more in a matter of an hour or so – often raw young wines – with a view to advising his employers how much to pay for a hogshead, having decided how many years it will be before they are ready to drink. He tastes in a clinically white-tiled tasting room, standing up to do so, rolling the wine round his mouth, and spitting out. The way for the likes of us to taste is to taste wines ready to drink, by the glassful and with food, which is how we want to enjoy them anyway. Best of all, is to have a bottle apiece of two or three examples of the same sort of wine – of claret, say, or burgundy, or dry or sweet whites – and have a few friends in for a meal or a wine-and-cheese buffet. You will soon decide for yourself which you like best, or which goes better with this sort of food, and which with that.

Labels

LABELS CAN BE CONFUSING, AND DIAGRAMS PURPORTING TO EXPLAIN them more confusing still. Suffice it to say that the laws of the EEC require a label to show where the wine comes from, how much of it the bottle holds, and by whom it was shipped and bottled. In addition, there are four categories of wine, and the label must indicate which category the wine comes under, if any:

1 Simple table wine from a non-EEC country;
2 Quality table wine from a non-EEC country;
3 Simple table wine, described according to the language of the EEC country it comes from as *vin du pays*; *täfelwein*; or *denominazione di origine semplice*;
4 Quality wine from an EEC country, strictly controlled as to methods of production, provenance and name.

France's top fifteen per cent or so of wines are AOC (*appellation contrôlée*) and her next fifteen are VDQS (*vins delimités de qualité supérieure*);
   Italy has DOC (*denominazione di origine controllata*) and the very rare DOCG (*denominazione di origine controllata e garantita*);

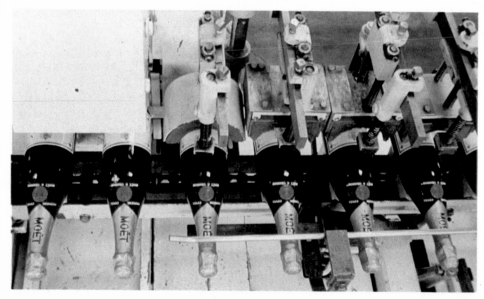

Labelling bottles of champagne. This process is usually carried out in the winter, before packing the bottles for shipment.

Champagne bottles come in many different sizes, but the distinct shape remains the same, the result of much research into how best to make the bottle resistant to the pressure inside it.

Germany has QbA (quality wine with a site-name) and QmP (quality wine with an extra qualification, such as Kabinett, one rank higher than QbA; Spätlese, meaning from grapes gathered after the general vintage for the sake of extra ripeness; Auslese, from specially selected bunches of grapes; Beerenauslese, from specially selected berries, overripe, to give great sweetness; and the luscious dessert wine Trockenbeerenauslese, from overripe single grapes that have been attacked by 'noble rot' (which is rare and expensive).

Just as there are fashions in wine – look at Beaujolais nouveau – so there are fads and fancies, some based on mere mumbo-jumbo. Take, for instance, the people who come back from their holidays enthusing about some local wine that they drank in a village in Provence or the Dordogne but, of course, 'you can't get it in England: it won't travel'. First of all, it was probably not a particularly good wine at all. It seemed delicious at the time because it was right for the local food. It was probably served young and fresh before it had time to develop faults (only really good wine improves with age; and most things taste better on holiday, anyway, and especially in the wine-growing countries).

The local grower may have said that his wine would not travel, the truth being that he sold all he produced each year to the local hotels and restaurants, and was not going to upset his old customers for the sake of some London shipper who might buy it for a year or so and then go elsewhere. How, then, would he get his old customers back? Or, perhaps, the returning traveller asked his own wine-merchant about the little wine he had fallen in love with and was told that: 'Oh yes, the man behind the counter knew *all* about it, but it won't travel.' What he really meant was that it was probably pretty poor stuff anyway, only worth drinking on the spot; that shippers and merchants cannot visit every vineyard in Europe, but rely on people they have dealt with for years, and that what he looks for in a wine is consistency both of quality and of supply. Especially what he means is that if he did set out to get this particular wine for this particular customer, he would have to buy a cask of it – getting on for three hundred bottles. Suppose the customer bought one bottle, or even one case of it, and then decided that he did not like it so much at home as in France?

Wine is a living thing and some wines, it is true, like some people, need a rest after a journey. This is especially true of some red wines with bottle-age, where there is a deposit that has to settle down after being shaken, and of some very delicate white wines that lose finesse if left lying about in barrels on docksides, though they travel reasonably well in bottle or in glass-lined containers. But any well-made wine with enough alcoholic content will be none the worse for a journey, and rough young wines come to no harm at all. The French are great ones for picnics, as any summertime traveller in France can see for himself, and an immense amount of French wine has to travel, and probably in the boot of an old rattletrap at that. Naturally, the picnickers do not take the most delicate clarets or the noblest burgundies for their days out, but the simplest district wines – just the wines, in fact, that our would-be know-alls tell us 'won't travel'.

How to Store Wine

THERE MAY STILL BE HIGH-BORN, OLD-ESTABLISHED WINE-LOVERS who are invited by their family wine-merchant to a glass of madeira and a biscuit in the parlour behind his shop to discuss the laying-down of a pipe of port (which is one hundred and fifteen gallons) or a hogshead of claret (which is two hundred and eighty-eight bottles). I am not one of them, nor do I believe that many of my readers are. We buy largely from hand to mouth, and if we keep a cellar at all it will be a modest one, for wine to be drunk in the fairly near future, and with friends and neighbours in mind as guests, not future generations. Nor need it even be a cellar as such. It need be nothing more grand than a cupboard under the stairs.

The late Raymond Postgate, who founded the *Good Food Guide*, once observed that 'wine is like a baby – it's a lot tougher than anxious parents think'. He went on to quote a relative who kept his wine under the bed, where it came to no harm. Then there are the French wine-growers who discovered a cache of fine old claret under a pile of the local gas company's coke. 'Coke has the most putrid and penetrating fumes: they were about to job the lot off at bargain prices when one of the more cautious vignerons drew the corks from three sample bottles. They were superb.' Bearing in

ABOVE *One way of storing wine cheaply: simply lay a crate on its side.*

BELOW *Most wine merchants sell simple wine racks like this, which are ideal for storing a small collection of bottles and will fit almost anywhere.*

mind, then, that most wines, especially the reds, will stand a fair amount of maltreatment, let us say that ideally the basic requirements for keeping wine in good heart are an equable temperature; an equable amount of light, preferably little or none; and stillness.

The ideal temperature for storing wine is around 55 degrees Fahrenheit, but red wines can be kept at 65 or so and come to no harm, save that they will develop more quickly. It is violent change that is harmful. I am bound to record, though, that when I was in Moscow in the winter of 1950–1, I imported some Château Talbot 1943 that arrived with tiny icicles in the bottles. The water content had frozen while the wine was awaiting collection at the customs warehouse. It thawed out in my almost excessively centrally heated hotel bedroom, and proved excellent. So pretty well any cupboard will do for red wine. White and rosé should be kept in the coolest place in the house – the larder if there is one – but not the fridge, except for an hour, in the least cold part of it, before serving. Never put white wine in the freezer, which would freeze all the character out of it.

Most wine-merchants sell wine-racks that hold bottles horizontally, so keeping the corks moist, as they should be, lest they shrink, and let in air, which oxidises wine. Bottles of spirits, though, should be kept upright. Gin, vodka and whisky rot corks.

A cellar of wine performs two functions. It provides an immediate reserve for day-to-day drinking and entertaining, and it enables one to buy fine wine young and cheap, or relatively cheap – no fine wine is really cheap. It can then be kept until ready to drink, when it would be dearer, or even unobtainable, at a wine-merchant's.

For day-to-day drinking do not despise red wines from countries other than France. The finest French reds are incomparable, but plenty of pretty poor stuff from France is sold at higher prices than its quality warrants because of the prestige earned by its betters. It is not for nothing that France is the biggest importer of North African and Italian wines. Many of the thin wines of France's deep south need the stiffening provided by these muscular foreigners. Sound Moroccan, Tunisian and Algerian reds, as well as Italian and Chilean, are fairly easily available and, as they are sold cheaply with small profit margins, wine-merchants cannot afford to put them away to acquire greater mellowness with bottle-age. Taste one bottle and keep others for even a few months, and see the difference.

I do not advise keeping many whites. The charm of all but the very greatest sweet Sauternes, hocks and the noblest – and most expensive – dry white burgundies lies in their freshness and youth. Unless you want a few bottles in reserve, buy as you need them. What goes for still white goes for sparklers. Keep, perhaps, a couple of bottles of non-vintage champagne, if you can afford them, against some unexpected cause for celebration – champagne keeps very well. If not champagne, then keep one of the cheaper sparkling wines mentioned in the chapter about sparklers, and buy others as needed. Keep a bigger stock, though, if, like me, you prefer a glass of fizz before a meal to sherry or a mixed drink based on gin or vodka. A husband and wife can enjoy a modest glass of fizz every evening for pretty well a week on one bottle – cheaper than a gin-and-something, and less trouble.

114

Serving Wine

The ideal corkscrew has a thread that
is neither too narrow nor too sharp, or
there is a danger that the middle of the
cork will crumble into a hole, from
which the corkscrew pulls out
ineffectively.

Removing the Cork

FIRST DRAW THE CORK. EITHER CUT AWAY THE TOP OF THE CAPSULE covering the cork with a sharp knife, or tear it away altogether. Use a corkscrew with a wide thread and a smooth edge. A narrow thread and a sharp edge reduce the middle of the cork to crumbs. A good wine-waiter uses a folding device like a penknife with a blade for the capsule, a corkscrew to be driven into the cork, and a lever to draw it out. But the best kind for the man or the woman who is his or her own butler is the French boxwood type with two butterfly handles – the small one at the top screws in and the bigger one below screws out. The bottle is upstanding all the time, and is not shaken about. As near as possible to being foolproof.

A sparkling wine is another matter. To point it at anything damageable, such as a mirror or a friend's face, is dangerous. To make the cork pop is vulgarly ostentatious. To open it without restraining the cork is likely to cause a mess. So, after taking off the wire muzzle by twisting the little loop, hold the cork with one hand and the bottle with the other. Then, *twisting the bottle, not the cork*, as soon as the cork is felt to be rising restrain it. It will ease itself out with a gentle sigh. Practice makes perfect, and provides a good excuse for opening a few bottles. If the cork is stubborn, hold the neck of the bottle under the hot-water tap for a second or so. If the top of the cork breaks off (which it shouldn't if you have followed my advice to twist the bottle, not the cork) pierce the rest of the cork with a skewer to release pressure before using an ordinary corkscrew. But keep the bottle wrapped up in a napkin – there will be a brisk burst of fizz.

In a restaurant and, ideally, in the home, the first few drops are poured into the host's glass, so that he gets any tiny bits of cork afloat on the top. Also so that he can smell the wine, and make sure that it is not 'corked'. Little bits of broken cork do no harm. Cork is tasteless, or we would not keep our fine clarets and vintage ports for years in the cellar with the wine touching the cork, to keep it moist. So a fragment of cork in the glass does not mean that the wine is 'corked'. 'Corkiness' is a vile, fungus-like smell arising from a faulty or diseased cork, the disease is caused by a weevil that lies dormant in cork. It is unmistakable, and so rare that you may never come across it in a lifetime of wine-drinking.

A slightly musty smell from an oldish bottle, that disappears after a few seconds in the glass (give it a chance before deciding that it is corkiness) is another matter. This is 'bottle-stink', found in old wines, and arising from the fact that the tiny amount of air between wine and cork has been there undisturbed for years, and needs refreshing. This is one of the many good reasons for decanting old wine, of which more later.

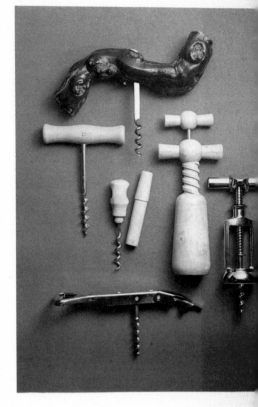

Different types of corkscrew: TOP *the basic shape, topped by an ornate handle;* EXTREME LEFT *the most basic kind of corkscrew;* CENTRE *a collapsible corkscrew;* RIGHT *these two corkscrews work in essentially the same way; the butterfly handles help to draw the cork gently, leaving the wine undisturbed;* BOTTOM *the French wine-waiter's corkscrew, complete with lever and penknife.*

OPPOSITE ABOVE *Modern wine glasses. From left to right: the tulip-shape, ideal for champagne, or indeed for any wine; two glasses of varying shape for red or white wine; a 'Paris goblet'; and a tasting glass (the bowl-shape retains the bouquet, and the funnel channels it up towards the nose).*

OPPOSITE BELOW *Antique wine glasses. Gilt and enamelled glasses by Giles of London and Beilby, 1765–80.*

Wine Glasses

WHAT YOU DRINK YOUR WINE OUT OF IS AS IMPORTANT AS THE WINE you drink. Try the wine you like best out of a glass and out of a chipped enamel mug. For that matter, champagne tastes very different in a glass from the way it tastes in the silver mugs used by some old clubs. This does not mean that wine-glasses need to be very fine and very expensive, though very fine glass is nice to have and to look at. What is important is that the glass should be reasonably thin and colourless. There should be a stem, so that when it holds cool white wine, the wine is not warmed by having to be cradled in the hand. It should be tulip-shaped, narrowing – or, at any rate, not widening – towards the top, to hold in the bouquet of the wine. A glass that holds a quarter of a bottle when full to the brim is ideal for any red or white table wine, and should be filled no more than half or two-thirds full at a time, so that there is room for the bouquet I mention. Such a glass can be found at any department store or supermarket. Anything grander is self-indulgence.

The same glass will do for sparkling wine, though a taller, more slender shape shows off the bubble better. To be avoided are the shallow, saucer-like Victorian glasses, like inverted *tutus*, which the French call *coupes*, fit only for ice-cream sundaes. They expose too much of the wine to the air, and bubble and fragrance disappear too quickly.

The only other glasses one needs in the sideboard are smaller versions of the kind I mentioned, for port and sherry, and very small balloons – small enough to be cradled completely in the hand – for brandy and liqueurs. The vast balloons, used in the flashy sort of restaurant that warms them for brandy over a spirit-lamp, are suitable only for goldfish.

Those who take their wine at all seriously must take washing-up seriously, too. It is not only a matter of appearance but also a matter of taste. A table of glittering glass looks splendid, whereas fingermarked glass looks squalid. A whiff of the washing-up water will ruin a fine wine. So can the smell of a glass that is perfectly clean, but that has been too long upside-down in a cupboard, catching and keeping a musty smell from the shelf it has been sitting on. Even a speck of dried detergent left in a glass has a harmful effect – so it is with soap, or a drop of water. Pour champagne into a perfectly clean but slightly wet glass and see how the bubble dies. Use detergents, by all means, whether at the sink or in a machine, so long as you are sure that the glasses are rinsed, and cloth-dried afterwards. (Some say that it is better to dry with kitchen paper.)

Decanters and Decanting

DECANTERS? BY ALL MEANS. OLD, FINE RED WINES NEED TO BE TAKEN off from the deposit that has formed in their bottles, and to free them from the bottle-stink already mentioned. Cheap young reds, too, are all the better for an airing that will take the edge off them as the stream of wine passes from bottle to carafe or decanter. The difference between a carafe and a decanter is that the decanter has a ground inside neck for the stopper; the carafe does not.

It is nice to have inherited fine Georgian decanters. Otherwise, buy plain modern ones to suit your own taste. Decanting itself is easy. Pour a young wine straight from bottle to carafe, but with an old wine let it stand upright

for some hours in the dining-room, so that the deposit settles at the bottom, then pour slowly, with the bottle between yourself and the light, ideally using a candle-flame or a small naked electric light bulb behind the shoulder of the bottle. A silver wine-funnel with a detachable strainer is an elegant device to have, but an enamel or plastic kitchen funnel, with a coffee filter paper or some clinically clean muslin will do as well. As soon as any deposit is seen moving from the shoulder of the bottle to the neck, stop pouring, leaving the contents of the decanter 'bright'.

Basket cradles are really meant for cellar use – to bring the bottle from the rack in which it has been lying horizontally to the decanter without changing its angle too much and thus disturbing its deposit. They should be used in restaurants only if the customer has given the wine-waiter no time to decant in the cellar; only if the wine is old enough to have formed a deposit; and only if the waiter pours as carefully into each glass as he would into a decanter, and empties the bottle at one serving. Otherwise, if he ups and downs it to refill the glasses he is merely washing the deposit up and down and making sure that it is in suspension in everyone's glass. Usually, therefore, the cradle is a meaningless affectation.

OPPOSITE *Old bottles and wine from Tarragona. Not all wine bottles need look as dusty as this.*

LEFT *A sophisticated type of decanter, in silver-mounted green glass, made in 1901.*

BELOW *Two Bordeaux wines accompany a tempting dish of cutlets.*

White wine does not need decanting. The only deposit it throws, and that rarely, is some little crystal-like flakes, which do no harm. But there are the cheap Italian carafes and the expensive silver-mounted German jugs mentioned in a previous chapter, that have separate containers for ice, to keep the wine cool and, as all wine looks prettier (especially rosé) in clear glass than in its bottle, they are pleasant things to have.

The wine left in bottles after decanting goes to the kitchen, for cooking and for marinading. This is the cook's department, not mine, so I quote from a piece my wife wrote in a book we did together about wine and food:

The best way to do this is to keep two half-bottles – or, better still, a couple of the screw-top bottles that hold soda or tonic – one for red, the other for white. I suggest small bottles, as the less air-space there is in the bottle the longer the wine will keep in good heart. . . . These bottles can be topped up with new nub-ends – a mixture of wines won't hurt for this purpose, and no one wants to go out and buy wine specially for cooking if there is some already in the house.

Wine adds richness to any number of dishes, both sweet and savoury; can be used with herbs and oil as a marinade, to tenderise and flavour dry meat; and a small amount added to the gravy of a plain roasted joint greatly enhances the flavour.

And, let me add, wine in the dish goes well with wine in the glass: *bon appétit!*

Acknowledgements

The photographs in this book were supplied and are produced by kind permission of the following (numbers refer to page numbers):

Peter Baker: 62

Barnaby's Picture Library: 100

Behram Kapadia: endpapers, 10, 26, 40, 76, 89, 108 (left), 113 (bottom), 113 (top), 115, 116 (top), 117, 119, 121

Cooper–Bridgeman Library: 116 (bottom), 121 (top)

Daily Telegraph Colour Library: 24

Douglas Dickins: 34–5

Graham Finlayson: 60

Food from France: 20 (bottom), 31, 41, 59

Guy Gravett: 12, 27, 30, 66, 107

Sonia Halliday: 14, 83, 85, 90 (top and bottom)

Robert Harding Associates: 23, 28, 120

Michael Holford: 13, 15, 16 (left), 19, 63, 65, 77, 78

Italian State Tourist Office (E.N.I.T.): 73

Marks and Spencer Ltd: 108 (right)

D. C. Money: 104

O.D.F., Paris: 111, 112

Pictor International: 93, 96, 102

Picturepoint: 6–7, 20 (top), 21 (bottom), 25, 37 (bottom), 38, 70, 71, 74, 88, 94, 101, 103, 110

Salins du Midi: 109

Ronald Sheridan: 16–7, 84

Spectrum: 8, 21 (top), 32, 38, 79, 82

Zentrale Farbbild Agentur: 4, 37 (top), 106